Things stand outside of us, themselves by themselves, neither knowing aught of themselves, nor expressing any judgment. What is it, then, which does judge about them?

—**Marcus Aurelius,** *Meditations*

SUBJECTIVITY & REDUCTION

An Introduction to the Mind-Body Problem

BARBARA HANNAN

University of New Mexico

WESTVIEW PRESS

Boulder • San Francisco • Oxford

Copyright © 1994 by Westview Press, Inc.

Published in 1994 in the United States of America by Westview Press, Inc., 5500 Central Avenue, Boulder, Colorado 80301-2877, and in the United Kingdom by Westview Press, 36 Lonsdale Road, Summertown, Oxford OX2 7EW

Library of Congress Cataloging-in-Publication Data
Hannan, Barbara.
    Subjectivity and reduction : an introduction to the mind-body problem / Barbara Hannan.
        p.   cm.
    Includes bibliographical references and index.
    ISBN 0-8133-1996-X. — ISBN 0-8133-1997-8 (pbk.)
    1. Philosophy of mind.   2. Mind and body.   I. Title.
BD418.3.H36   1994
128'.2—dc20   93-49474
                                                                                                       CIP

Printed and bound in the United States of America

⊗   The paper used in this publication meets the requirements
    of the American National Standard for Permanence of Paper
    for Printed Library Materials Z39.48-1984.

10   9   8   7   6   5   4   3   2

For John Heil,
who introduced me to the mind-body problem

Contents

Preface

ONE OF MY MOST deeply held convictions is that philosophy is for all thinking persons, not just for the few who endure graduate programs in philosophy. More often than is necessary, books on philosophical problems are written strictly for a professional audience and are difficult or impossible for the beginning student or interested non-philosopher to understand. This opacity stems not from any intrinsic difficulty of the subject but rather from the use of specialized terminology that goes unexplained.

In this book, I have made every effort to explain specialized philosophical terminology whenever such terminology is used. I do not presuppose that the reader has any background in philosophy, though the later chapters may be more challenging than the earlier ones. It is my hope that the book will serve as a reasonably accessible introduction to the mind-body problem while at the same time being sufficiently non-elementary to be of interest to graduate students and professionals.

I have made no attempt at neutrality; in this book I criticize views I take to be wrong and defend views I take to be right. Some of my views are controversial, but I believe these controversial elements should add to the book's appeal rather than detract from it.

An instructor who wishes to assign this book in a course will find it most useful in combination with some of the readings I cite. A recent anthology edited by Brian Beakley and Peter Ludlow, *The Philosophy of Mind: Classical Problems, Contemporary Issues* (Cambridge: MIT Press, 1992), contains many of the readings I cite in its excellent sections on the mind-body problem and mental causation. I recommend Beakley and Ludlow's anthology as a companion volume to my book. My book devotes considerable attention to eliminative materialism and to non-reductive materialism, two topics not specifically addressed in Beakley and Ludlow's anthology; Beakley and Ludlow include readings on mental imagery, associationism/connectionism, and innate ideas, topics my book does not mention. Despite this lack of complete overlap, the two books together could be used to teach an excellent course on the philosophy of mind.

Barbara Hannan
Albuquerque, N.Mex.

Acknowledgments

THIS BOOK has a checkered past. When I first started working on the manuscript, it wasn't clear to me whether I was trying to write an introduction to the mind-body problem or a monograph presenting my own views. I thought I was finished many times before I really was finished. My greatest debt is to a few conscientious philosophers who read early drafts of the manuscript, pointed out my mistakes and confusions, and gently steered me in the direction of an introductory treatment of the issues. In this respect I am particularly grateful to John Heil and to Kirk Ludwig, whose help was above and beyond the call of duty. I am also grateful to Christopher Maloney and Lynne Rudder Baker. Keith Lehrer deserves special thanks; without his prodding and encouragement I never would have written this book. To Spencer Carr, editorial director at Westview Press, I extend my gratitude for his comments as well as for his belief in the potential of my manuscript.

Subsequent drafts were read by Robert Audi and Fred Schueler, both of whom provided excellent suggestions. Ned Block generously read Chapter 3, on functionalism, and offered valuable comments. Jaegwon Kim, ever since I attended his summer seminar on supervenience in 1990, tried to get me to stop chasing certain red herrings regarding multiple realization, type identity, and supervenience; I finally saw the light, and I thank him for that insight.

The seeds of this book were planted when I was a graduate student at the University of Arizona. Various bits of the text are taken from my doctoral dissertation (University of Arizona, 1989). I extend general thanks to those who taught me philosophy of mind in graduate school: Stephen Schiffer, John Pollock, Mike Harnish, and Rob Cummins. I would also like to thank the National Endowment for the Humanities, which provided me with a fellowship during calendar year 1992, enabling me to work on the book. I had the stimulating experience of spending my fellowship year at the University of California at Berkeley. I wish to thank John Searle for sponsoring me as a visiting scholar in the Berkeley philosophy department and for his advice and encouragement. I am also grateful to Donald Davidson, who provided me with comments on an early draft of Chapter 6 while I was at Berkeley.

Parts of Chapter 6 previously appeared in *Mind* (vol. 99, April 1990, pp. 291–297), in the context of my critical notice of Daniel C. Dennett's *The In-*

tentional Stance. I would like to thank the editors of *Mind* for permission to use that material.

Finally, I would like to thank some people dear to my heart who kept me sane and solvent during the writing of this book: my parents, William S. Hannan and Nancy B. Hannan; my sister, Elizabeth Hannan; my brother, Paul Hannan; and my friend George Patsakos.

B. H.

1

The Mind-Body Problem
and Substance Dualism

ONE'S LIFE, from beginning to end, is a sequence of subjective experiences. Because we are so utterly accustomed to being selves, unified centers of subjectivity, we seldom pause to reflect on how mysterious and intriguing is this phenomenon of subjective consciousness. Sometimes, however, perhaps in a moment of extraordinarily intense subjective experience, the wonder of being a conscious self can strike a human being with compelling force.

I recently had such an experience. I was in the middle of a long car trip from northern California to southern Arizona. On the road between Barstow and Needles, the desert and the mountains began to look peculiarly beautiful to me. I was playing some quiet, atmospheric music on the cassette player and reflecting on some recent good fortune. The scenery, the music, and my generally pleased state of mind combined to produce a temporary euphoria. A feeling of great happiness washed over me like a wave. At the very moment of experiencing this wave of joy, it occurred to me: How strange it is that there is an *I* who experiences this. Here is this organism, responding to various sensory stimulations and neural memory traces. Somehow, this organism experiences itself as a unified subject. There is a *person*, a *self*, to whom a wave of joy happens here, and not just a collection of neurons and muscles and electrochemical impulses. Why should this be so? What makes it so?

This is, in its most naked form, the mind-body problem. We know that we have minds; we have mental lives consisting of feelings, thoughts, memories, urges, obsessions, qualms, and so on. We also know that we have brains, nervous systems, and physical bodies. What, precisely, is the relationship between the mental being and the physical being?

What happens when we think or feel? Something goes on in the brain, surely. But does something go on as well in another place, the mind? When we look at brains we see masses of neural tissue. When we look through a microscope we see the tiny, cellular components of this tissue. We never catch a glimpse of a feeling, or a thought, or an urge, however. Yet such

1

things make up the fabric of our subjective lives. Where are these mental things? Does it even make sense to ask?

Reflective individuals have been trying to say something illuminating about the mind-body problem for thousands of years. Until roughly the 1700s, there were no clear dividing lines among the disciplines we now call empirical science, psychology, and philosophy. Thinkers who called themselves 'philosophers' freely speculated on the possible relationships between mind and body and suggested principles to systematize and explain what goes on within consciousness. Nowadays, the philosophy of mind has become distinct from biological science and from psychology.

Neurobiologists, acting on the (well-justified) hypothesis that the activity of the brain gives rise to the phenomena we call 'mental', investigate how the brain and nervous system work, seeking some clue as to how this horrendously complicated mass of 'wetware' produces consciousness. Psychologists, also proceeding from the modern assumption that the relationship between mind and brain is a very intimate one, concentrate upon finding the principles and mechanisms governing the inner, subjective lives of persons. Philosophers tend to concentrate their attention on conceptual difficulties that arise from the fact that our ways of thinking and talking about persons are inherently dualistic, despite the mind-brain unity that has become scientific orthodoxy.

This is the fact upon which philosophers concentrate: We describe persons and explain their behavior in two ways. On the one hand, a person is taken to be a biological organism, the behavior of which is explainable in terms of events in its environment and in terms of physical goings-on in the brain and nervous system. On the other hand, a person is taken to be a subjective self, a rational agent with a point of view and purposes who performs actions for reasons and is responsible for his or her behavior. Just how these two conceptual schemes or descriptive/explanatory vocabularies mesh is less than clear. It is this latter, peculiarly philosophical, mind-body problem that is treated in this book.

Before the philosophical mind-body problem can be discussed in any detail, it is necessary to set aside a certain widespread and almost certainly mistaken view of the nature of the mind: substance dualism. Substance dualism is the idea that every person is composed of two distinct substances—a physical substance (the body) and a mental substance (the mind or soul).

We live in a time when two views of the nature of persons, fundamentally incompatible with each other, are both widely accepted (often by the same individuals, who somehow remain blissfully unaware of the inconsistencies within their own thoughts). I mean the view of the nature of persons taken by physical science and a more ancient view of the nature of persons associated with many traditional religions.

Children in contemporary America, for example, grow up being taught in school that human beings, like other animals, are complex physical organisms, their nature and behavior based in biological, chemical, and physical processes. (Call this the scientific view.) But the same children are taught in church, and by various sources in the popular culture, that human beings are fundamentally non-physical souls or spirits; these spirits inhabit the physical body and are released from it upon death. (Call this the substance dualist view. Notice, the substance dualist view is not *necessarily* associated with religion.) The irreconcilable conflict between these two views is obvious if one devotes barely more than passing thought to the matter.

The scientific view is that life, consciousness, and rational thought are phenomena that have evolved in certain complex physical systems; these phenomena arise from the functioning of those physical systems. Scientists operate on the faith that, in time, we will fully understand the nature of these phenomena. When the physical system deteriorates or is damaged and ceases to function, life and mental phenomena cease; the individual consciousness that once characterized that organism is no more. The self or individual consciousness of an organism can no more continue to exist after the organism dies than the running of an automobile can continue to exist after the engine is switched off or melted down. The substance dualist view suggests that human life, consciousness, and rational thought are properties of a substance or entity separable from the physical organism. When the human body deteriorates or is damaged and ceases to function, the person's life, consciousness, and rational thought may go on, because the spirit leaves the body and goes elsewhere. Human life, consciousness, and rational thought are not functions of material substance, but something wholly different, and physical science will never be able to discover and understand their nature.

It is often held, as a part of the substance dualist view, that other animals, unlike human beings, do not have this spiritual nature; other animals cease to exist upon death, but not human beings. This is absurdly *ad hoc*, as many small children naively realize when they ask whether the soul of a deceased pet will go to heaven. More consistent than their elders, such children can see that there is no fundamental biological distinction between human beings and other kinds of animals, and they draw the reasonable conclusion that if the life and consciousness of one sort of animal is due to the presence of a soul, as they have been told, then so must be the life and consciousness of other sorts of animals. They are understandably confused (or outraged, as I remember being) when told that this is not so. As I recall, it was this sort of consideration that first led me to be suspicious of my parents' Christian religion. It cannot be that both the substance dualist view and the scientific view of the nature of persons are true. One view asserts what the other explicitly denies. These two views of the nature of persons are irreconcilably at odds with each other. I shall now argue that the scientific view is rationally prefer-able.

When two theories compete for our allegiance, it is good methodology to prefer the theory with greater explanatory power. The scientific view of the nature of persons explains much that the substance dualist view does not.

For example, the scientific view explains why persons with damaged brains cannot think as well as persons with undamaged brains: It is the brain's normal functioning that constitutes thinking, and when the brain can no longer function normally due to structural damage, of course thinking will be substandard. The competing, substance dualist view cannot explain the effects of brain damage upon thinking. If it is the non-physical soul or spirit that thinks, why can't it think just as well in a damaged brain as in an undamaged brain? After all, the soul is supposed to be able to think *without any brain at all.*

The scientific view also explains why mental functioning develops ontoge-netically right along with the physical development of the brain and nervous system. Fetuses, babies, and small children possess characteristic levels of mental functioning, lower than the levels of mental functioning possessed by adults, and these levels coincide with the degree of development of the brain. Again, the substance dualist view cannot explain this; the soul is supposed to inhabit the body at some point, at which point the body should presumably possess full mental functioning. There are degrees of mental development, and they appear to depend upon degrees of physical development. For the substance dualist view, this must remain a mystery.

The scientific view, similarly, can explain why mental capacities appar-ently developed phylogenetically in tandem with brain development. If men-tal functions are just brain functions, then it makes perfect sense that early hominids with less sophisticated brains were not so bright as more evolu-tionarily advanced hominids with more sophisticated brains. How is the substance dualist view going to explain this? Did early hominids just happen to have unsophisticated souls, this fact having no relation at all to their de-gree of brain development? The substance dualist view cannot even explain why humans and dogs have more powerful minds than grasshoppers and liz-ards. After all, it is supposed to be the non-physical soul that has the think-ing power. Why should it be the case that the best-thinking souls always in-habit the bodies with the most highly evolved brains?

Not only does materialism regarding minds have great explanatory power that spiritualism lacks, the assumption that having a mind is just having a functioning brain has brought about much successful research and useful re-sults. Certain forms of mental illness, such as depression, have proven to be treatable by drugs that affect brain chemistry. The drug Prozac, for example, successfully alleviates depression in many individuals by inhibiting the brain's reuptake of the neurotransmitter serotonin. Surely, to think that such effects are just coincidence stretches credibility to the limit.

Some people suggest, methodological considerations such as the above aside, that there is empirical evidence of the existence of non-physical souls or spirits. For example, it is commonly asserted (by beginning philosophy students, among others) that so-called 'out of body experiences,' including near-death experiences, constitute such evidence. Let us evaluate this suggestion.

Let us assume for the sake of argument that it is empirically well established that 'out of body experiences' do occur *as subjective phenomena.* Suppose that people of many different cultures, ages, and backgrounds, when exposed to certain types of physical trauma, report remarkably similar subjective sensations of 'floating' over their bodies, moving disembodied through space, and so on. The question is, Does the existence of such subjective phenomena lend any logical support to the claim that minds are non-physical spirits?

Not much. Because people can have hallucinatory subjective experiences, the mere report of a subjective experience does not by any means establish that the experience portrays the reality of what is happening. Compare: Suppose it is established that cocaine addicts of all ages and cultures report remarkably similar subjective experiences of bugs crawling all over their bodies. Does it follow from this that cocaine addicts really do have bugs crawling all over their bodies? Of course not. All that follows from the phenomenon of 'cocaine bugs' is that the physical trauma of cocaine addiction sometimes has a certain effect that manifests itself psychologically as the illusion that bugs are crawling on the body. Likewise, all that follows from the phenomenon of 'out of body experiences' is that certain physical traumas (perhaps heart stoppage, oxygen deprivation, the ingestion of certain psychoactive drugs, etc.) sometimes have effects that manifest themselves psychologically as the illusion that one's consciousness is floating disembodied.

What *would* qualify as serious empirical evidence for mind-body dualism? This is an interesting question, because some dualists assert that the mind is a *non-physical substance* that has no weight or mass and takes up no space. Such a substance could not possibly register on any instrument or be empirically detectable in any way.

Compare the situation with the cocaine bugs. What would constitute serious empirical evidence of the actual existence of bugs crawling on the skin of cocaine addicts? If we could capture such bugs and observe them, weigh them and measure them, record their attributes, and so on, that would count. Of course we cannot do that; cocaine addicts experiencing 'cocaine bugs' have no unusual observable or capturable creatures crawling on their skin, even if we look with our best microscopes. But suppose the advocate of the actual existence of cocaine bugs asserts, "Cocaine bugs are very special bugs. They are non-physical. They take up no space; they have no weight and no mass. They are detectable only from the subjective point of view. Nevertheless, they have real and objective existence."

If cocaine bugs are presumed to be invisible to objective observers and not detectable by physical instruments, then no possible empirical evidence could qualify as evidence of cocaine bugs' existence. This is why we don't believe in the actual existence of cocaine bugs and consider the bugs to be a subjective phenomenon only: There is no actual or possible physical evidence of the existence of the bugs.

Many people reject the hypothesis of non-physical minds, souls, or spirits for similar reasons; there is no physical evidence of the existence of such minds. There are no observations that we need the hypothesis of non-physical minds to explain. All of our observations can seemingly be explained more simply and more coherently with the hypothesis that the mind is just the functioning brain. The plea of those who persist in believing in non-physical minds, souls, or spirits is no better than the plea of our fictional eccentric who persists in believing in cocaine bugs: "Minds are very special things. They are non-physical. ..." Why should we believe in these 'very special' entities? Their existence appears to be an unnecessary hypothesis.

The substance dualist, however, may argue that he has an ace up his sleeve. He may argue that there are convincing *a priori* reasons to believe in the existence of non-physical souls or spirits, whereas there are no convincing *a priori* reasons to believe in the existence of cocaine bugs.

It is necessary at this point to digress briefly and explain the philosophical distinction between *a priori* reasons and *a posteriori* reasons. Both sorts of reason are rational considerations (premises) in support of some conclusion. *A posteriori* reasons are evidential in character, drawing upon experiment and observation. *A priori* reasons are conceptual in character, drawing upon what one can know without making observations about the external world.

As an example of an *a posteriori* argument, consider the following. Faraday observed that whenever a magnetic field changes in the presence of a conductor, an electric current is generated in the conductor. Faraday drew the conclusion that this must be a law of nature: Whenever there is a changing magnetic field in the presence of a conductor, an electric current is generated in the conductor. Notice that Faraday's argument depends on his observations of the behavior of magnetic fields, not on any 'armchair' analysis of the concept of a magnetic field.

By contrast, consider the case of Saint Anselm's *a priori* argument for the existence of God. Anselm argued as follows: It is part of the very concept of God that God is the greatest being that can be imagined. A thing is greater if it exists in reality than if it merely exists as an idea in the mind; this follows from the concept of greatness. Therefore, God must exist in reality. Notice that Anselm does not predicate his argument on any observed evidence at all;

he proceeds by analyzing the concepts of God and greatness, by appealing to what everybody can be expected to know who has mastered these concepts. (One must not conclude that all *a priori* arguments are fallacious on the basis of Anselm's example.)

What would constitute an *a priori* reason to believe in the existence of non-physical minds, souls, or spirits? René Descartes thought he had such reasons. In his *Meditations on First Philosophy*, Descartes argues as follows:

> ... because I know that all the things that I clearly and distinctly understand can be made by God exactly as I understand them, it is enough that I can clearly and distinctly understand one thing without the other in order for me to be certain that the one thing is different from the other, because at least God can establish them separately. ... For this reason, from the fact that I know that I exist, and that meanwhile I judge that nothing else clearly belongs to my nature or essence except that I am a thing that thinks, I rightly conclude that my essence consists in this alone: that I am only a thing that thinks. Although perhaps (or rather, as I shall soon say, to be sure) I have a body that is very closely joined to me, nevertheless, because on the one hand I have a clear and distinct idea of myself—insofar as I am a thing that thinks and not an extended thing— and because on the other hand I have a distinct idea of a body—insofar as it is merely an extended thing, and not a thing that thinks—it is therefore certain that I am truly distinct from my body, and that I can exist without it.[1]

Descartes offers an additional argument for substance dualism:

> ... there is a great difference between a mind and a body, because the body, by its very nature, is something divisible, whereas the mind is plainly indivisible. Obviously, when I consider the mind, that is, myself insofar as I am only a thing that thinks, I cannot distinguish any parts in me; rather, I take myself to be one complete thing. Although the whole mind seems to be united to the whole body, nevertheless, were a foot or an arm or any other bodily part amputated, I know that nothing would be taken away from the mind; nor can the faculties of willing, sensing, understanding, and so on be called its 'parts,' because it is one and the same mind that wills, senses, and understands. On the other hand, no corporeal or extended thing can be thought by me that I did not easily in thought divide into parts; in this way I know that it is divisible. If I did not yet know it from any other source, this consideration alone would suffice to teach me that the mind is wholly different from the body.

Call these two arguments, respectively, Descartes's first and second arguments for substance dualism. Do these arguments have any force? Let us examine them one at a time.

Descartes's first argument for substance dualism is somewhat difficult to understand without some familiarity with the *Meditations* as an entire work. Descartes argues in the earlier sections of the *Meditations* that God exists and is not a deceiver.[2] Such a non-deceptive God, according to Descartes, would not allow his creatures to be led into error by careful use of their most 'clear and distinct' modes of reasoning, such as mathematical reasoning and deductive logical reasoning.[3] Following up on these ideas, Descartes argues for substance dualism roughly as follows: Mind and body clearly have different conceptual essences; the essence of mind is to think, the essence of body is to be extended. Since mind and body have this 'clear and distinct' logical difference, and God would not allow us to be deceived with regard to what we so 'clearly and distinctly' conceive, mind and body must really be distinct substances.

Descartes's first argument for substance dualism is not very convincing. From the fact that mind and body have different conceptual essences, it may follow that mind and body are not *necessarily* the same substance, but it does not follow that mind and body are not in fact the same substance. Consider an analogy. Barbara Hannan is not necessarily the same person as the author of *Subjectivity and Reduction*. Being Barbara Hannan is conceptually or essentially distinct from being the author of *Subjectivity and Reduction*. We can clearly conceive of (imagine) a situation in which Barbara Hannan is not the author of *Subjectivity and Reduction*. Nevertheless, as a matter of contingent fact, Barbara Hannan is the author of *Subjectivity and Reduction*.

Descartes's first argument for substance dualism fails because he attempts to draw a factual conclusion (mind and body really are distinct substances) from a modal premise (mind and body are possibly or conceivably distinct substances). Even if God exists, it is apparent that he allows us to imagine or conceive many possible scenarios that do not reflect the facts. Descartes's conception of his mind existing apart from his body could be one of those vivid but false imaginings.

Descartes's second argument for substance dualism is perhaps more interesting. He argues that bodies are divisible and minds are not divisible; therefore, bodies and minds cannot be the same substance. This argument, unlike Descartes's first argument for substance dualism, at least appears on the surface to be valid (if the premise were true, it looks as if the conclusion would follow logically). And, at least on one reading of the premise, the premise is true: It does seem that there is something conceptually incorrect in speaking of minds being divisible into parts in the same way that bodies are divisible into parts.

The argument's superficial appearance of validity, however, is deceptive. Suppose we give Descartes's premise the (plausible) reading just suggested: There is something conceptually odd about speaking of minds being divisible into parts in the same way that bodies are divisible into parts. Does it follow that mind and body must be two distinct *substances*? No; all that follows is that the concept of mind is not logically analogous to the concept of body. The concept of a mind is the concept of a set of capacities for intelligent behavior. Sets of capacities may be divisible in a certain sense (it is possible to possess some but not all of the set), but a set of capacities cannot be cut up with a knife, as a physical structure can. This logical difference between the concept of mind and the concept of body does not, however, mean that the two concepts refer to separate substances. Brains, or whole living persons, could be purely physical structures possessing the mental capacities at issue. If this were the case (and I believe it is the case), then we would have two conceptual schemes with two separate logics, but both conceptual schemes would refer to one and the same physical substance.

Descartes's second argument for substance dualism, then, is as doubtful as Descartes's first argument for substance dualism.

Descartes is not the only famous philosopher who has argued for substance dualism. Plato, in his dialogues, puts various arguments for substance dualism in the mouth of Socrates. One of these Socratic arguments for substance dualism, occurring in the *Meno* dialogue,[4] is interesting enough to be worthy of our attention.

In the *Meno*, Socrates demonstrates that a slave boy who has never been taught mathematics possesses enough native mathematical intuition to answer correctly a lot of questions about a geometry problem. Socrates' diagnosis of the situation is that the slave boy somehow knows a lot about mathematics without being taught; questioning serves to bring out knowledge that is already in the boy's mind. When we come to possess knowledge in this life, according to Socrates, we are merely recollecting what we already knew. Since knowledge is not originally acquired in this life, Socrates reasons, it must be acquired in a former existence, either in some other incarnation or when the soul is disembodied.

In effect, Plato's Socrates uses the doctrine of knowledge as recollection to argue for mind-body dualism. We need not accept that the soul is a separate entity from the body unless we accept the premise that there is no true learning in this life but only recollection of knowledge absorbed in past lives. It is hard to see why one would feel compelled to accept such an odd premise. It remains an open possibility that genuine learning does occur in our lives and that such native capacities as mathematical intuition can be explained in biological terms rather than in mystical terms. If non-mystical explanations can be given of the acquisition of human knowledge, then the Platonic motivation to be a substance dualist vanishes.

There remains one other popular argument for mind-body dualism, which might be called the argument from free will.

The proponent of the argument from free will is apt to say something along the following lines: "The hypothesis that the mind is just the brain has unacceptable consequences. Suppose that the mind is just the brain. Then, all mental states are physical states of brains, including the mental states that cause the sort of voluntary behavior we call free action. Whether a particular physical state of the brain will come about is due to a long series of physical causes, a series extending to environmental events outside the control of the agent. Accordingly, whether a particular bit of so-called voluntary behavior will occur is also due to a long series of physical causes, a series extending to biological and environmental causes outside the control of the agent. If this is the case, then all of our behavior is causally determined by factors beyond our control; so-called voluntary behavior is not really voluntary, people do not really perform free actions, and no one is responsible for anything he or she does. This is unacceptable; we do perform free actions, and we are sometimes responsible for what we do. Therefore, the mind must be something besides the brain; the mind must be a non-physical substance, free of the physical causal nexus, that makes undetermined decisions to perform voluntary acts and is wholly responsible for the resultant acts." One short answer to the argument from free will is simply to deny than we have free will; the dualist is not entitled to assume that we do. Even if it is granted that humans have 'free will' in some sense of that term, the argument from free will still fails. 'Free will' can be understood to mean something compatible with the physical causation of human action.

From the premises that minds are brains and mental states are brain states, it does not follow that people don't perform free, voluntary actions and that people are not responsible for their actions. Sorting out this particular variety of confusion, and explaining why it is wrongheaded, has been the project of theorists called compatibilists or soft determinists who write about the philosophical problem known as the problem of free will and determinism.[5] My primary concern in this book is the mind-body problem, not the problem of free will and determinism, but in order to defeat the argument from free will for mind-body dualism I must conduct a brief foray into the free will and determinism problem. I shall briefly explain compatibilism and why I take it to be the correct position.

According to the compatibilist, the existence of free action and the correct ascription of moral responsibility for action are compatible with its being the case that humans are wholly physical organisms whose behavior is subject to exhaustive causal explanation in terms of physical states. When we say that a given action was freely done, we do not mean that the action had no physical causal chain leading up to it. Rather, we mean that the action was not the result of force, constraint, pathology, or relevant mistake of fact. We mean that the chain of physical events leading up to the act had certain features and lacked certain other features, not that the physical causal chain was gappy or wasn't there.

The compatibilist holds that decisions regarding which actions are free and which are unfree, and decisions regarding who is and is not responsible for actions, are made quite without regard to the question of whether action is causally determined. Such decisions are made on the basis of the answers to questions, like: Did the agent have the normal capacities to understand the nature of his behavior and to conform his behavior to his intentions or was he suffering from some disease or other physical condition that interfered with these capacities? Was the agent under the influence of any psychoactive substance, and if so, was the ingestion of that substance voluntary or involuntary? Was the agent acting under some relevant mistake of fact, and if so, was his mistake reasonable? Was the agent's action the result of his own desires and intentions, or was the agent being forced by someone else to behave contrary to his own desires and intentions? And so on.

Notice that the question is never, Was the agent's behavior caused by some chain of physical events? but rather, *What* chain of physical events caused the agent's behavior in this case, and were any of these physical causes relevantly unusual? Notice that this is the way responsibility is regarded in criminal law and tort law. The compatibilist suggests that holding one another responsible for certain types of normally produced behavior is a socially useful practice. Since normal individuals have the capacity to foresee that they will be held responsible, morally and legally, for certain sorts of conduct, the existence of moral and legal sanctions serves as a causal factor that influences behavior, in general, for the good of society. We decline to hold persons responsible where, for one reason or another, there would be no social usefulness in holding them responsible (as, for example, in the case of insane and retarded persons who lack the capacity to be deterred from conduct by the prospect of sanctions). These social practices having to do with action and responsibility may plausibly be taken to presuppose that actions result from chains of physical causes. At the very least, these practices do *not* presuppose that action is *not* the result of such physical causal chains.[6]

There will be individuals who will maintain, at this point in the discussion, that the compatibilist view of freedom and responsibility is counterintuitive. I can only reply that I do not find it so. I find it vastly more intuitive than its competitors, one of which is the (wild, I think) proposal that people never perform free actions and are never responsible for what they do, and the other of which is the mysterious idea that agents are non-physical, spiritual things that somehow cause or causally influence particular physical events. One reason that the latter idea strikes me as so counterintuitive is the so-called interaction problem: If the mind really is a non-physical thing, how does it manage to cause physical events in the brain and body? How do two such different substances interact?

My experience is that the substance dualist, faced with the interaction problem, usually offers the following counterargument: Causal interaction between physical things is just as mysterious as causal interaction between physical things and non-physical things. We do not understand any kind of causal interaction, so mind-body causal interaction presents no *special* problem.

This point has some force; causal interaction of any kind is mysterious. But it does seem methodologically troublesome to take one mystery and add another to it. Isn't one sort of mysterious causation, physical-physical causation, enough, without positing another sort of mysterious causation, mental-physical causation? It would seem preferable to eschew a proliferation of mysteries unless we really need an additional mystery to account for something important. Since there exists an account of free action and responsibility compatible with it being the case that there is only one sort of causation, physical-physical causation, I submit that there is no reason to admit a mysterious new variety of causation into the picture. The conclusion appears inescapable: The rational course is to abandon the substance dualist view of the nature of persons and embrace the scientific view of the nature of persons, with its ontological materialism. We cannot have it both ways, and there are overwhelming evidential and methodological considerations weighing on the side of science and materialism. It is only when the specter of substance dualism has been exorcised that serious work on the mind-body problem can begin.

Let the reader be assured, I am not advocating a crude scientism, according to which we must turn to science to answer all our questions. Philosophy has its place. Conceptual and metaphysical questions present themselves to the human mind as worthy of answers, yet these are not scientific questions, as they cannot be answered by appeal to observation and experiment. (Actually, even scientific questions properly so called cannot be answered purely by appeal to observation and experiment, but I will put that point aside for our purposes.)

We would not turn to science to answer a normative question, such as 'What principles would govern a just society?' Such questions are properly addressed by philosophical ethics, which takes a rigorous, analytic approach to the analysis of concepts such as justice and right action.

There are other conceptual questions besides normative questions, and other branches of philosophy besides ethics. Science itself depends on such notions as that of justified belief, well-confirmed theory, truth, rationality. Epistemology, logic, and philosophy of science investigate such concepts, seeking a deeper understanding than is sought by scientists, who presuppose these notions without analysis.

Nor can science answer the metaphysical questions that arise in the periphery of even the most successful empirical theories. Quantum mechanics, for example, makes strikingly successful probabilistic predictions regarding the measured behavior of subatomic particles, but quantum mechanics cannot tell us what is really happening in the subatomic world between measurements; the latter is a metaphysical question to which the mind of a curious scientist irresistibly turns, even if the scientist is nominally of the positivist bent that officially eschews speculation into matters beyond what is directly observable and measurable.

Philosophy begins where science ends, and science surely ends before all interesting questions are answered. The question of whether there exists a special mental substance, however, has been satisfactorily answered by science, or so I have argued. Having an appropriately functioning brain is sufficient to have a mind; no substance but physical substance is necessary. Materialism has won the day, and remaining philosophical problems concerning the mind arise within a materialist framework.

2

Reductive Materialist
Mind-Body Theories

NOW THAT IT IS CLEAR that substance dualism is not a tenable solution to
the mind-body problem, we may move on and consider mind-body theories
that have, at various times, been taken to be promising materialist solutions.
Materialism, as I will use the term, is a thesis regarding what objects, entities,
and substances exist; materialism asserts that all objects, entities, and substances are physical (made of physical stuff). Before the leading materialist
mind-body theories can be presented, it is unfortunately necessary to introduce some specialized vocabulary and philosophical distinctions. Here I ask
the reader's forbearance. The following, while it may seem to be a boring di-
gression into philosophical jargon, will help in understanding what comes
later.

SOME IMPORTANT TERMINOLOGY
AND DISTINCTIONS

When we consider an organism as having a mental life, we use a peculiar set
of concepts to describe the organism and explain its behavior. We describe
the organism as having *mental states,* and we explain much of the organism's
behavior by reference to those mental states. Philosophers have traditionally
divided mental states into two basic types: *qualitative states,* such as perceiv-
ing a color or feeling a pain, and *propositional attitudes,* such as believing
that the mind-body problem is interesting or desiring that one's pet parrot
should learn to talk. Both types of mental state have *content,* in different but
related senses of the word 'content'.[1] The content of a qualitative state is a
privately felt sensation; these private sensations are sometimes called *qualia.*
The content of a propositional attitude is characterized in language by
means of a that-clause. Both notions of content have this in common: Both
express something that is part of the subjective, inner life of a sentient being.

It is important to say a bit more about propositional attitudes. Included
among propositional attitudes are beliefs, desires, hopes, fears, doubts, in-

tentions, and so on. Such states are called propositional attitudes because to have such a state seems to involve the agent in taking an attitude toward a proposition. Consider, for example, the following proposition: *There is a roadrunner in the yard.* If I have no thoughts about roadrunners in the yard at a given time, then I am taking no attitude at all toward this proposition. I may, however, on different occasions, believe that there is a roadrunner in the yard, wish that there were a roadrunner in the yard, doubt that there is a roadrunner in the yard, intend to put a roadrunner in the yard, fear to find a roadrunner in the yard, and so on. Notice how all these mental states involve taking different attitudes (belief, desire, doubt, intention, fear) toward the proposition that there is a roadrunner in the yard.

Propositional attitudes, and the sentences that ascribe them, have features that have been intriguing to philosophers. Propositional attitudes are *intentional* states; that is, they are about something, they are representational. This sense of the word 'intentional' is a philosophical term of art and should not be confused with the sense of 'intentional' meaning done on purpose.

Certain contexts within sentences ascribing propositional attitudes to persons can be *intensional*. 'Intensional', spelled with an 's', is another philosophical term of art and should not be confused with either sense of 'intentional'. In order to understand what it is for a context within a sentence to be intensional, consider the following pair of sentences:

A1. Oedipus marries Jocasta.
B1. Oedipus desires that Jocasta should be his wife.

Sentence A1, which does not ascribe a propositional attitude, contains names occurring only in non-intensional (extensional) contexts; if the sentence is true, we can substitute co-referential terms for the names and the sentence remains true. For example, we could change sentence A1 to

A2. Oedipus marries Oedipus's mother.

The sentence retains its truth-value (truth-values are just the two possible states, being true and being false) so long as the terms we substitute have the same reference. When such truth-saving substitution of co-referring terms within a sentence is possible, that sentence is said to have an extensional context.

By contrast, consider what happens when we substitute a co-referring term for the name inside the that-clause in sentence B1, the propositional attitude ascribing sentence. We get

B2. Oedipus desires that Oedipus's mother should be his wife.

Obviously, sentence B1 could be true, and sentence B2 could be false, even though the terms 'Jocasta' and 'Oedipus's mother' have the same reference. Contexts in which substitution of co-referring terms fails to preserve truth are said to be intensional contexts.

The intensional nature of some contexts within propositional attitude ascribing sentences may seem at first glance to be an abstruse point having nothing to do with the mind-body problem. Examples like the above seem to show only a rather obvious fact: Our beliefs about certain individuals may be mentally indexed under particular descriptions, and we may not in some cases realize that two different descriptions in fact refer to the same person. So what?

The importance of the point about the intensionality of certain contexts within propositional attitude ascribing sentences lies in the following: Our theories regarding the nature of minds and mental states are themselves propositional attitudes; a theory is just a certain kind of belief. Our theories regarding natural phenomena, like our beliefs about individual persons, come before our minds with their subject matter cloaked in certain concepts or descriptions. The concepts and descriptions under which we tend to think of mental phenomena may turn out to refer to something we initially did not anticipate. Just as Oedipus discovered that the sexually desirable Jocasta was in fact the sexually taboo mother, we may discover that our ineffable, subjective mental states are in fact 'effable', objective brain states.

To put this another way: The point about the intensional nature of contexts within propositional attitude ascribing sentences calls attention to a crucial distinction between the *reference* (denotation) of a term and the *sense* (connotation) of the term.[2] This distinction is important in the philosophy of mind when we begin to consider the project of *reduction*. The notion of reduction may be illuminated by considering some examples.

Once, lightning was not known to be identical with an atmospheric electrical discharge. Modern science, however, has shown us how to understand lightning in terms of electrical discharges, and so reduced the former to the latter. Similarly, it was once unknown that a gas's having a certain temperature was just the gas's molecules possessing a certain kinetic energy. But this discovery was eventually made. Temperature in a gas was thus reduced to a physical property, the property of having a certain kinetic energy of molecules.

Prior to the relevant empirical discoveries, there were competent users of the concepts 'lightning' and 'temperature in a gas'. But no amount of intuitive analysis of the sense or connotation of these concepts could yield knowledge of the natural properties to which these concepts turned out to refer. 'Lightning' and 'temperature in a gas' turned out to be *natural kind concepts,* concepts that refer to physical properties, mind-independent properties of the world describable in the language of physical science.[3]

Some theorists in the philosophy of mind have been deeply impressed by this phenomenon of property reduction.[4] They have gone so far as to suggest that mental concepts (such as the concept of being in a given qualitative state or a given propositional attitude state) must, like lightning and temperature in a gas, turn out to designate physical properties; otherwise, mental concepts have no legitimate application and must be eliminated from serious descriptions of the nature of sentient beings. In what follows, I will refer to this orientation as *the reductionist/physicalist ideology*. Implicit within this ideology is the conviction that natural kinds are the only kinds that may legitimately enter into serious descriptions and explanations.

A confusing but unavoidable complication is created by the fact that philosophers often use the word 'reduction' for any complete and non-circular analysis or explanation of a concept in terms of better-understood or more legitimate concepts, even when the explanation does not amount to the discovery that a given concept refers to a physical property. I follow general practice in often using 'reduction' in this more broad sense. When I specifically intend the narrower sense, I use the term 'the reductionist/physicalist ideology'.

In order to understand reduction in either of its senses, one must grasp the distinction between *types* and *tokens*. Failure to do so has led to endless confusion and philosophical grief. A token state or event is a dated, non-repeatable, individual occurrence. A type, in contrast, is a *kind* of state or event or entity. The word 'desk' stands for a type of entity. 'My desk' refers to a particular token of this type. The demand for reduction of a concept is the demand for a non-circular account of a given type (kind). Tokens are not properly described as being subject to reduction.

Other distinctions that must be kept in mind are those among *properties, concepts,* and *predicates*. A predicate is an expression in language that can be combined with a singular referring term to yield a sentence (for example, 'is red'). A concept is what is expressed by a predicate and what we understand in understanding the predicate. Corresponding to the predicate 'is red' is the concept of being red. A property is what we attribute to an object when we apply a predicate to it. For example, in saying that my shirt is red, I attribute to my shirt the property of being red.

THE MIND-BODY PROBLEM AS THE SEARCH
FOR A REDUCTION

Many philosophers these days think that there is no problem regarding the nature of mental state tokens and mind tokens. It is accepted by such token materialists that (on this planet, anyway) mind tokens are brain tokens[5] and that mental state tokens are brain state tokens.[6] A problem does exist, however, regarding the nature of mental properties or concepts (types).

This is the essential reductive issue that constitutes the mind-body problem as discussed in recent philosophy: What is it to be in a given qualitative state or in a given propositional attitude state? What is true of a creature in such a state, in virtue of which it is true to describe the creature as being in that state type?

To make the issue more graphic: Suppose I find myself in certain mental states on September 5, 1992, at two o'clock in the afternoon. I find myself experiencing a dull, throbbing pain in my right ankle. I recall spraining my ankle on the stairs in Moses Hall a few days before, and the belief crosses my mind *that the stairs in Moses Hall are slippery.* At the relevant time, I have an ankle pain, and a belief that the stairs in Moses Hall are slippery. A materialist will take these to be physical state tokens of my brain and nervous system. But what is the nature of the types or properties at issue? What is it to have a dull, throbbing pain in one's ankle? What is it to believe that the stairs in Moses Hall are slippery? Are there facts (physical facts, behavioral facts, or some other sort of facts) that constitute being in these mental state types?

Let us look briefly at two leading attempts to reduce mental concepts and examine the reasons why many philosophers have concluded that these reductive ventures were failures. The two reductive approaches I will discuss are

1. Reductive physicalism (type identity theory).
2. Logical behaviorism.

REDUCTIVE PHYSICALISM
(TYPE IDENTITY THEORY)

In the 1950s, several philosophers defended the thesis that consciousness and sensations were just processes in the brain, in exactly the sense that we take lightning to be just an electrical discharge or heat to be just mean molecular kinetic energy.[7] They argued for this materialist identity theory in the face of certain conceptual arguments that were then widely taken to establish that mental states could not possibly be identical with physical states.

These conceptual arguments are now of interest largely for their value in learning to avoid a certain kind of fallacy. Consider an example of the sort of argument at issue:

1. I know that my belief that I am less than six feet tall is about me.
2. It is not the case that I know that brain state B is about me.
3. Therefore, brain state B is not identical with my belief that I am less than six feet tall.

This argument as it stands is invalid. The idea behind it would be to argue that if brain state B were identical with my belief that I am less than six feet tall, we could substitute 'brain state B' for 'my belief that I am less than six feet tall' in premise 1 and get the negation of premise 2. But since the context following 'know that' is intensional, substitution of co-referring terms is not guaranteed to preserve truth. So this argument is not valid.

To see more clearly what is going on, consider an analogous argument having nothing to do with mental states and brain states:

1. Oedipus knows that Jocasta is in Thebes.
2. Oedipus does not know that his mother is in Thebes.
3. Therefore, Jocasta cannot be identical with Oedipus's mother.

This obviously fallacious argument is parallel in logical form to the mind-brain argument above, and this enables us to see that the form of the mind-brain argument is logically suspect.

The arguments of the 1950s-era identity theorists pointed to the important distinction (discussed previously) between the sense or conceptual meaning of a referring term and the object it refers to. Even if mental state terms don't have the same connotation as brain state terms, suggested these philosophers, they might after all turn out to have the same denotation (just as 'Jocasta' and 'Oedipus's mother' turned out to have the same denotation).

The discussion spawned by the ideas of these early identity theorists eventually made clear that the mental state/brain state identity theory could be interpreted in two different ways. It could be interpreted as a type identity theory or as a token identity theory.

The token identity theory amounts to the claim that individual mental states in this world happen to be physical states as a contingent matter, even though this identity is not necessitated by any essential aspect of mental properties. Mental states might have turned out not to be physical states (substance dualism might have been true), but as a matter of fact, mental states did turn out to be physical states. The token identity theory is not an especially exciting or controversial claim.

The type identity theory is the stronger claim that mental properties, as a matter of discovered natural necessity (what Saul Kripke has called 'necessary *a posteriori* truth[8]), will turn out to be physical properties.

The distinction between token identity and type identity may be illuminated by examples. As an example of token identity without type identity, consider pawns in chess. Every pawn is identical to some bit of physical reality, as a matter of contingent truth, but having a realization in physical stuff is not *essential* to pawnhood; there might be non-physical chess sets in some other possible world (heaven, perhaps). We cannot identify the property of being a pawn with the disjunctive property composed of all the physical state types that realize pawnhood on different occasions in our world. The property of being a pawn is not identical with any physical property, even though every pawn is, in our world, realized in some physical state or other. The property of being a pawn is a functional property, not a physical property.

Compare the case of pawns with the case of water. Every bit of water is, we have discovered, a bit of H_2O.[9] And this is *not* just a contingent identity; *water could not have turned out not to be H_2O*. This is because our word 'water' expresses a natural kind concept; it was originally defined by pointing at a certain substance and saying (the equivalent of) "*That stuff*, whatever its nature is, shall be called 'water'.*"* In Saul Kripke's terms, the word 'water' *rigidly designates* for us a particular chemical compound, H_2O. The property of being water (that which is ascribed when something is taken to fall under the concept 'water') is the property of being H_2O.[10]

This point about necessary *a posteriori* truths is apt to strike readers as counterintuitive. Can't we easily imagine that water turned out not to be H_2O? Surely we can imagine that the stuff in the lakes and rivers turned out to be some other chemical compound. But notice: When we imagine such cases where, seemingly, water turned out not to be H_2O, what we imagine are cases where something else, not water, was called 'water'. The word 'water' in our mouths necessarily expresses the property of being H_2O, because of the way that word is tied to our physical environment *as that physical environment actually is*.

The property of being water, then, is identical to the property of being H_2O. This is a natural necessity we discovered. The type identity theorist predicts that particular mental properties will be discovered to be necessarily identical to particular (simple or disjunctive) physical properties, just as the property of being water was discovered to be necessarily identical to the property of being H_2O.

The type identity theory is often taken to demand that a given mental property must turn out to be identical with a single, non-disjunctive physical state type. This is a mistake, stemming from an old and outmoded conception of what constitutes a genuine property reduction.[11] When this error is made, however, it looks as if the type identity theory can be attacked using the so-called multiple realization argument. The proponent of the multiple realization argument argues, "It just does not seem likely that all the people who are in a certain mental state (say, all the people who believe that Jaegwon Kim is intelligent) are in precisely the same type of brain state. *Believing that Kim is intelligent* would seem to be more like *being a pawn* than like *being water*; it seems likely that different people's beliefs that Kim is intelligent will have different physical realizations, just as pawns from different chess sets have different physical realizations. Further, it is surely possible that future computing machines, or creatures from some other planet with silicon-based nervous systems, might appropriately be described as believing that Kim is intelligent, and they can't possibly share brain state types with humans, since they do not have brains like our biological brains. The type identity theory as applied to propositional attitude states such as beliefs must therefore be false."

The type identity theory as applied to qualitative states such as pains is also commonly taken to be vulnerable to the multiple realization argument: "It just does not seem plausible that every creature that is in pain (be it human, frog, horse, shark, lobster, or whatever) is in exactly the same type of physical state."

Multiple realization, however, is a red herring as an argument against the type identity theory. Current conceptions of property identity (reduction) allow a given higher-level property to be identical with a complex, disjunctive physical property. A good example is the reduction of temperature. Temperature is one property in solids, another in gases, another in plasmas, and so on.[12] Still, we take the property of temperature to be identical with the disjunction of these physical properties. Mental properties might, in similar fashion, turn out to be identical with disjunctions of physical properties. In short, type identity and multiple realization could both be true; there is no conflict between them.

Jaegwon Kim defends type identity theory as the only way to secure scientific legitimacy for mental properties. According to Kim, science classifies properties by their causal powers, and mental properties (if they have any genuine causal powers) presumably inherit their causal powers from the physical properties that realize them.[13] It seems we must *identify* mental properties with their physical realizations if we want mental properties to be real; reality of a property, for Kim, presupposes that the property has *independent* causal powers.

Kim's argument in favor of type identity theory is powerful. There is, I believe, only one way for an opponent of type identity theory to reply to Kim and Kim's reductionist brethren. An argument must be mounted that mental properties cannot be identical with physical properties *because mental properties are essentially subjective;* this subjectivity renders mental properties *sui generis,* irreducible to anything described in objective terms. (The opponent of type identity theory would then presumably want to argue that such subjective properties are real features of the world, even though subjective properties possess no causal powers independent of the causal powers of the physical properties that realize them on particular occasions—see Chapter 8.)

Saul Kripke has made such an argument.[14] Kripke uses pain, a qualitative mental property, as his example. According to Kripke, if pain were identical with some brain state type, this would have to be a necessary *a posteriori* identity, like the identity of water with H_2O. The word 'pain', therefore, would have to be used in such a way that it rigidly designates a certain brain state type, just as the word 'water' is used so that it rigidly designates a certain chemical compound. But we don't use the word 'pain' to rigidly designate a certain brain state type; we use 'pain' to rigidly designate a certain *sensation,* an essentially subjective phenomenon. The word 'pain' does not mean a certain natural kind in the way the word 'water' means a certain natural kind. The meaning of the word 'pain' is tied not to our physical environment as it actually is but to *what we feel as beings with a subjective point of view.* The property of being in pain, therefore, cannot be identified with the property of being in a certain type of brain state.

Could an argument akin to Kripke's be used to show that propositional attitude properties, like qualitative properties, are essentially subjective and therefore not identifiable with physical properties? I believe so; as previously mentioned, I take subjectivity to be the common feature that unites qualitative and intentional mental properties as *mental.*

Those who are persuaded by arguments such as Kripke's that mental properties are essentially subjective and therefore irreducible tend to endorse the idea that mental properties *supervene on* physical properties as opposed to being identifiable with physical properties. A higher-level characteristic is said to supervene on a base set of physical properties when the presence of that higher-level characteristic depends on the presence of one or another of the physical properties in the base, *but the higher-level characteristic cannot be identified with its physical base.* (The underlying base set of physical properties is said to be *subvenient.*)

Supervenience first appeared in the philosophical literature in connection with ethical properties such as goodness. It was said that such evaluative properties supervened on, but did not reduce to, descriptive properties. The absence of a genuine reduction was supposed to stem from the fact that no descriptive property could ever be identical with a normative (evaluative) property. Despite the lack of property identity, descriptive properties were taken to *determine* evaluative properties in the following sense: Two things could not be alike in all descriptive properties yet differ in their evaluative properties.[15] That is, if Saint Francis is good, someone exactly like Saint Francis in all descriptive respects must also be good; if a given act of cat burning is wrong, a descriptively exactly similar act of cat burning must also be wrong.

Mental properties may be seen as similar to moral properties in the following respect: Mental properties have an aspect that cannot be captured by specifying the physical properties that may realize them on particular occasions. Mental properties are subjective, and subjective properties can no more be captured by objective descriptions of physical states than evaluative properties can be captured by value-neutral descriptions. In other words, the peculiar mentalistic vocabulary in which we describe humans as persons with mental states has unique connotations of subjectivity, and it is not clear that a purely neurophysiological vocabulary would have these essential connotations.

If this line of argument succeeds, there is a principled reason why reductive mind-body theories tend to fail; mental properties are indeed *sui generis* in their subjectivity and not candidates for identification with objective properties of any kind.

LOGICAL BEHAVIORISM

Another attempt to reduce talk of mental states to some more scientifically respectable form of discourse is known as *logical behaviorism*. Logical behaviorists offer a simple, straightforward solution to the mind-body problem. My having a thought or a pain is simply a matter of my behaving in certain ways, my moving my body, uttering words, or my being disposed to do certain things.

Perhaps the best statement of logical behaviorism is that given by Gilbert Ryle in his book *The Concept of Mind*.[16] Ryle there develops logical behaviorism as a response to substance dualism; he refers to substance dualism as 'the dogma of the ghost in the machine'. He argues that to think of the mind as a place where thoughts occur, and to construe thoughts as coming prior to and directing action, is a 'category mistake'. A category mistake is the sort of mistake someone might make who has been shown the buildings, grounds, and students at a university and then says, "Well, I've seen the buildings, grounds, and students; now show me the university." Such a person imagines the university to be some other item on a par with a building, a quadrangle, or an undergraduate. Ryle thinks we make a similar mistake in taking mental states to be private, subjective items.

Ryle argues that if thoughts in some ghostly realm really came prior to, and caused, action, there would have to be an infinite regress of ghostly causes. (That is, if a ghostly thought causes an action, we would have to ask what causes the thought, what causes the cause of the thought, and so on. Since the original thought is taken to be in some ghostly, subjective realm, presumably its cause must also be in that realm, and so on.) He further argues that the thought (that it is going to rain, for example) *just is* certain behavior and dispositions to behave; mental language is just one sort of higher-level vocabulary in which we talk about overt, objective, physical goings-on (specifically, behavior).

While it is not clear that Ryle ever intended his theory to be construed this way, others took logical behaviorism to be the notion that mental state terms could be *operationally defined* in terms of behavior and behavior dispositions. An operational definition gives observable criteria for the application of a term. It provides a test in terms of something observable under hypothetical conditions. For example, 'water soluble' could be operationally defined as follows: 'X is water soluble if and only if, placed in water, X would dissolve'. In order for logical behaviorism to constitute a reductive thesis about the nature of mental concepts or properties, it seems that such operational definitions would have to be possible. Attempts to give behavioristic operational definitions of mental state terms failed, however.

Consider some simple examples. Suppose we try to define two mental state terms, 'feels thirsty' and 'believes it is going to rain' operationally, in behavioristic terms. We might try the following: 'X feels thirsty if and only if, when offered water, X would drink it'; 'X believes it is going to rain if and only if, when going out, he would take his umbrella'.

It doesn't take much reflection to see that such attempts are inadequate. You might feel thirsty yet refuse to drink water when it is offered: You might believe the water to be poisoned or you might be refusing to drink any liquids until the government grants independence to a certain province, etc., etc. You might believe that it is going to rain yet wouldn't take your umbrella if you were to go out: You might believe that it is bourgeois to carry an umbrella, and you might object to appearing bourgeois, etc., etc.

The general point is that the behavior dispositions one has, given that one is in a certain mental state, depend on what other mental states one is in.[17] It is impossible to define any particular mental state operationally, wholly in terms of hypothetically observable behavior, because of this fact. Even if we make attempted operational definitions very complex, they do not constitute reductions of mental state vocabulary to behavioristic vocabulary, because the definition always contains further mental state terms.

The main argument against logical behaviorism amounts to the following: You can't conclude from behavioral dispositions that the behaver has certain beliefs and desires, since other combinations of beliefs and desires—or even robot states with no content at all—could have produced the same behavioral dispositions. Ned Block points out that this line of argument doesn't work as well against the prospect of a behavioristic definition of *intelligence* as it does against the prospect of a behavioristic definition of individual beliefs and desires. It can easily seem that certain intelligent behavioral dispositions guarantee that the behaver is intelligent. A famous test, the Turing test, purporting to be a test of machine intelligence, appears to presuppose that behaviorist criteria suffice for intelligence. As part of our discussion of logical behaviorism, it will be worthwhile to look briefly at the Turing test to see why its behaviorist assumptions about intelligence are flawed.[18]

Alan Turing, one of the great pioneers of computer science, proposed the following test in 1950 for whether a computing machine could think: Suppose a judge is communicating by teletype with entities in two other rooms. The entity in one of the rooms is a person; the other entity, in the other room, is a computer. After carrying on teletype 'conversations' with each of the two entities for a specified period of time, can the judge tell which one is the person and which one is the computer? If not, the computer passes the Turing test; by Turing's criteria, the computer is genuinely intelligent.[19]

Block raises the following objection to the Turing test. If the test is intended to provide a behaviorist definition of intelligence, it contains a crucial gap: We are not told how the judge is to be specified.[20] Presumably, the judge is supposed to be intelligent; otherwise, what grounds would we have for accepting his or her judgments as to what constitutes a person and what constitutes a mere mindless machine? But if we specify the judge as being intelligent, or give some mentalistic criteria for the judge's intelligence, we have involved ourselves in a circular argument. The Turing test was supposed to define intelligence in non-mentalistic, purely behavioral terms. If we build a mentalistic construal of intelligence into the test, we have simply begged the question of how to define intelligence.

Block further points out that computer programs exist that pass the Turing test, but no one possessing the ordinary concept of intelligence would want to call these programs intelligent. One such example is ELIZA, a program designed to mimic a psychotherapist.[21] An account of ELIZA's canned responses to a patient's remarks is extremely amusing, especially if one has experience with real, human psychotherapists. Here is Block's account of how ELIZA works:

> ... it looks for "key words" on a list supplied by the programmer—say *I, you, alike, father,* and *everybody.* The words are ordered: for example, *father* comes before *everybody,* so that if you type in "My father is afraid of everybody," the machine will spit back one of its 'father' responses, such as "WHAT ELSE COMES TO MIND WHEN YOU THINK OF YOUR FATHER?" If you type in "Everybody laughed at me," you will get one of its responses to *everybody,* such as "WHO IN PARTICULAR ARE YOU THINKING OF?" It also has techniques that simultaneously transform *you* into *I* and *me* into *you,* so that if you type in "You don't agree with me," it can reply, "WHY DO YOU THINK THAT I DON'T AGREE WITH YOU?"[22]

An ordinary person might not be able to tell ELIZA from an actual psychotherapist under Turing test conditions. But we balk at concluding that ELIZA is intelligent. Why? Fairly obviously, because something more than canned responses to key words in one's utterances is required of a genuinely intelligent interlocutor. Intelligence demands that the interlocutor understand the entire utterance and respond appropriately to its meaning. ELIZA is not understanding anything, nor is ELIZA responding to the meaning of her interlocutor's utterances, despite her ability to pass Turing's behavioristic test. In ELIZA we have a counterexample to the notion that certain behavior dispositions can suffice for intelligence.

Logical behaviorism does appear to proceed from some correct insights. We do often use observable behavior as evidence for our ascriptions of mental states to others and even to ourselves. Ryle appears correct that it is a category mistake to take mental state talk as describing some mysterious non-physical realm. Logical behaviorism seems incorrect, however, insofar as it claims that mental states just are behavioral events rather than internal causes of such events, and it fails to provide reductive definitions of mental state concepts.

3

Functionalist
Mind-Body Theories

THE MOST POPULAR approach to the mind-body problem in recent years has been *functionalism*. Functionalism is not, strictly speaking, a materialist mind-body theory; it takes mental properties to be functional properties rather than physical or behavioral properties. As we saw earlier in connection with the functional property of being a pawn in chess, functional properties are not physical properties. Functional kinds could be realized in non-physical stuff in other possible worlds, even if they always happen to be realized in physical stuff *here*. The essence of a functional kind is not what it *is* but what it *does*.

Functionalism appears, at first glance, to combine the attractive features of reductive physicalism and logical behaviorism while avoiding their separate problems. We shall see, however, that functionalism arguably no more provides a successful account of the nature of mental properties than does either of its predecessors.

To believe that it is going to rain would be, on a functionalist characterization, to possess a token of some internal state type that has a certain functional property (plays a certain functional role). What functional role? Well, a belief that it is going to rain tends to be caused by sightings of clouds and by television weather reports, it may interact with a desire not to get wet so as to produce umbrella-carrying behavior, and so on.

This is really just Rylean logical behaviorism, but it explicitly resurrects Ryle's often-forgotten admission that mental properties are to be defined not just in terms of observable behavior and operationally testable behavior dispositions but also in terms of interactions with other mental states.

Recall that a certain mistaken objection to type identity theory accuses type identity theory of not allowing multiple realization of mental state types. Functionalism has been attractive to many because it avoids this putative implausibility of the type identity theory. Functionalism acknowledges that one mental state type may, in different organisms or even at different times in the same organism, be realized by different physical state types.

(This is not really an improvement on the type identity theory, as we have seen; type identity theory allows mental properties to be identical to disjunctive physical properties.)

Functionalism also avoids the putative implausibility of logical behaviorism by not demanding that mental state concepts be operationally definable in terms of behavior alone.

Functionalism, like type identity theory and logical behaviorism, is a reductive theory; it seeks to tell us what mental properties *are* in non-mental terms. Functionalism aspires to perform the reductive task by specifying the functional roles of mental state types. How the functional roles of given mental state types are supposed to be specified differs according to different versions of functionalism. Here we will examine three influential versions of functionalism: commonsense functionalism, Turing machine functionalism, and homuncular functionalism. The versions presented of commonsense functionalism and Turing machine functionalism are due respectively to David Lewis[1] and to Hilary Putnam.[2] Homuncular functionalism is a more broad research orientation that has been defended by, among others, William Lycan[3] and Kim Sterelny.[4] (Homuncular functionalism has earlier origins in the writings of Robert Cummins,[5] Daniel C. Dennett,[6] and Jerry Fodor.[7])

DAVID LEWIS'S COMMONSENSE FUNCTIONALISM

Lewis points out that theoretical terms often are implicitly defined by the sets of sentences in which these terms occur. Consider the term 'gene'. Before it was determined that genes were bits of DNA, it was known that *something* performed the task of encoding genetic information and passing it on to subsequent generations. The term 'gene' was coined to refer to whatever performed that task. At the time when 'gene' was such a theoretical term, it would have been possible to string together all the sentences uttered by scientists in which the term 'gene' occurred. The term 'gene' could have been replaced in these sentences by the variable x, and the entire string of sentences could have been prefixed with 'There exists a type of thing, x, such that ... .' The result would have been a device known as a Ramsey sentence (named for F. P. Ramsey, a British philosopher who invented the device). The Ramsey sentence would succeed in defining 'gene' as whatever, if anything, plays a certain functional role.

Lewis suggests that mental state terms such as 'belief that snow is white' and 'pain' are theoretical terms like 'gene', implicitly defined in the same way by their role in some theory. Of course, our theory of belief and pain is a commonsense, implicit theory rather than an explicit scientific theory, but the way the embedded terms are defined is the same, according to Lewis.

Suppose we could somehow articulate and string together all the true declarative sentences in which the term 'belief that snow is white' occurs. Then, suppose we replaced every occurrence of the term 'belief that snow is white' with the variable x and prefixed to this vast string of sentences the specification, 'There exists a state type, x, such that ... .' The result would be a Ramsey sentence implicitly defining the belief that snow is white as *whatever* stands in certain relations. The Ramsey sentence might read in part as follows: 'There exists a state type, x, such that Barbara has a token of x, and Barbara's token of x, along with Barbara's belief that grass is green, caused Barbara to say, "Snow is white and grass is green," and such that John has a token of x, and John's token of x, along with John's desire to ski, caused John to realize that he desired to ski on white stuff. ... ' This is crude, but the idea should be clear. Lewis's suggestion is that our commonsense, everyday use of mental state terms amounts to an implicit theory that there exist state types playing certain functional roles.

Lewis's version of functionalism is vulnerable to a certain objection. This objection concerns the application of this version of functionalism to qualitative states such as pain. According to Lewis's functionalism, pain is whatever plays a certain functional role, as specified by the sentences in which the term 'pain' occurs. Consider a simplified Ramsey sentence for pain: 'There exists a state type x such that tokens of x are frequently caused by damage to body tissues, and tokens of x, in the absence of inhibitory mental states, frequently result in anguished outcries, unhappy facial expressions, etc. ... ' The problem is the following: It seems easy to imagine a creature (or a machine) that responds to what we would regard as painful inputs (pokes with sharp objects, electrical shocks) with outputs we might consider appropriate (squeals, withdrawal, avoidance) and yet *feel* nothing at all. Intuitively, it seems that this creature is not in pain, though it meets criteria specified by Lewis's version of functionalism for being in pain.

This may seem to beg the question against a functionalist who might insist that to respond in the given way to such stimuli is just what it is to be in pain. This, however, misses the point of the example. We can give the functionalist all he or she wants, and still something is left out, namely, the qualitative character of our mental lives.

A similar problem plagues the attempt to state in functional terms what it is to experience a given color sensation. Suppose we wanted to give a functional characterization of the mental state *seeing red*. We might say that seeing red is the state that typically comes about when the creature views ripe strawberries, the predominant feathers of male cardinals, etc., and may result, given appropriate other internal states, in such events as verbalizations of "It's red." But this will not do. For, suppose that the given creature is a person with an inverted subjective color spectrum; this person, when exposed to ripe strawberries and to the predominant feathers of male cardinals, has the color sensation that you and I have when we look at newly sprouted grass and at the predominant feathers of Amazon parrots. Of course, the person with the inverted subjective spectrum calls this color sensation 'red', and there's no way we could ever detect the subjective difference in visual qualia. Still, intuitively, the person with the inverted subjective spectrum does not see red when he or she looks at ripe strawberries. And the functional definition of seeing red implies that the person with an inverted spectrum does see red when looking at ripe strawberries.

The objections we have been discussing to Lewis's version of functionalism are usually called, respectively, 'the absent qualia objection' and 'the inverted spectrum problem'. Qualitative states arguably are defined by reference to how they feel subjectively, not by the causal relations into which they enter, as implictly specified by our commonsense usage of qualitative-state terms.

HILARY PUTNAM'S TURING MACHINE FUNCTIONALISM

It should be noted that Putnam has gone through many phases with regard to his views on the mind-body problem. Putnam introduced Turing machine functionalism,[8] subsequently modified it,[9] and later retracted his allegiance to any form of functionalism.[10] The view attributed to Putnam in what follows should be recognized for what it is—a view adopted by Putnam at one point in his career and later reconsidered.

Putnam suggested that a mental state such as pain might be a Turing machine state. The functional role of pain could be specified by supplying a 'machine table' for the human Turing machine. Before we can understand this suggestion, we must familiarize ourselves with two notions: that of a Turing machine and that of a machine table for a Turing machine.

Alan Turing invented a certain abstract specification for a computer. Turing was able to show that, in principle, any formal system (any computable function) could be implemented by such a machine. Turing described the machine as consisting of certain components (a tape divided into squares bearing symbols such as os and 1s, and a device that can scan the tape, erase symbols on the tape, and write new symbols on the tape). The machine can carry out certain operations. It can move the tape one square to the right or to the left; it can rewrite a 0 on the tape as a 1, and it can rewrite a 1 on the tape as a 0. Turing's particular description of the machine is not essential, however. The key idea behind a Turing machine, for our purposes, is just that it is a device capable of being in certain states and capable of receiving certain inputs; the next state of the device, and its output if any, is always a function of its initial state plus the input it receives. The states, inputs, outputs, and state transitions undergone by a given Turing machine are specified by means of a diagram: the machine table for that Turing machine.

Look at Figure 3.1. The gumball machine described by the machine table in Figure 3.1 illustrates the basic idea of a Turing machine. The gumball machine can be in State One or State Two. It can receive nickel inputs or dime inputs. The state of the gumball machine at any given moment is determined by its initial state plus the input it receives.[11] The gumball machine is a *deterministic* Turing machine; the machine will definitely give you a gumball, provided it is in State One and you give it a dime, etc. If state transitions and outputs are not certain given initial states and inputs, but only follow with a certain degree of probability, the machine is a *probabilistic* Turing machine.

Putnam's suggestion was that we take a human being to be a very complex probabilistic Turing machine and that we take pain to be a state of that machine. (Turing machines are really special sorts of discrete state machines, and what Putnam describes is really a generalization of a Turing machine to include a greater variety of inputs and outputs.) Part of our machine table (the specification of our state/input/output function) might look like Figure 3.2. Note that State One corresponds to pain and State Two corresponds to non-pain. The machine table attempts to define these states in terms of their causal interactions, without making use of any mentalistic vocabulary.[12]

Putnam later realized that there were serious problems with the idea that mental states could be Turing machine states. A Turing machine can be in only one state at a time, whereas mental states (both qualitative states and propositional attitudes) are such that we are in many mental states all at once. Further, there is a disanalogy between Turing machine states and mental states when we consider the role of learning and memory in the constitution of mental states. A Turing machine can have learning and memory, but these are *inputs,* not states. Turing machine states are independent of learning and memory. But many mental states are partially defined by what we have learned and remember, for example, being jealous. In order to be jealous of my lover's former wife, I must know and remember many things about my lover and his former wife.[13]

In addition to these problems raised by Putnam, Turing machine functionalism appears vulnerable to the absent qualia objection and to the inverted spectrum problem. Specifying being in pain or seeing red as a Turing machine state is much the same as specifying being in pain or seeing red à la Lewis, in terms of these states' causal roles in various individuals. Any specification of a qualitative state in terms of its causes, interactions with other mental states, and effects is bound to leave out what is arguably the defining essence of a qualitative state: its subjective feel.

HOMUNCULAR FUNCTIONALISM

Homuncular functionalism is a research strategy in cognitive science that attempts to explain complex cognitive capacities, such as the ability to recog-

	STATE ONE	STATE TWO
Nickel INPUT	OUTPUT: Nothing. Go to State Two	OUTPUT: Gumball. Go to State One.
Dime INPUT	OUTPUT: Gumball. Stay in State One.	OUTPUT: Gumball and nickel; go to State One.

SOURCE: Adapted from Ned Block, "Troubles with Functionalism," in Brian Beakley and Peter Ludlow, eds., *The Philosophy of Mind: Classical Problems, Contemporary Issues* (Cambridge: MIT Press, 1992), p. 72.

FIGURE 3.1   Machine table of the Turing gumball machine.

	STATE ONE	STATE TWO
INPUT: Cuts made in skin.	OUTPUT: Cries of distress. Stay in State One.	Go to State One.
INPUT: Morphine.	OUTPUT: Idiotic grin. Go to State Two.	OUTPUT: Idiotic grin. Stay in State Two.

FIGURE 3.2   Part of the machine table of the human Turing machine.

nize a face or understand a sentence, by breaking such capacities down into less complex subcapacities. The idea is to explain intelligent capacities by showing how such capacities might emerge out of more basic, unintelligent computational processes.[14]

Suppose someone proposed the following theory: A human can recognize familiar faces in virtue of possessing a neural face-recognition system. Such a theory would be unhelpful, because the theory in effect posits a 'homunculus', a little person, inside a human being. In order to explain how the human being does something intelligent, it is proposed that there is another intelligent little human being inside the original human being. It isn't the original person who recognizes faces; it's his or her neural face-recognition system! Clearly, the positing of such homunculi makes no theoretical progress. What is wanted is an explanation of intelligence, not the positing of new, unexplained intelligence.

Homuncular functionalism seeks to solve this problem by breaking down a homunculus such as the neural face-recognition system into progressively less intelligent subcapacities. Perhaps there is a memory system that stores front and profile views. An executive system takes a particular visual input and classifies it as either a front or profile view. A library system matches the visual input with the possibilities stored in memory. The eventual output of all these interacting systems is the identification of the face.[15] Crucial to the idea of homuncular functionalism is that each of the subcapacities can itself be broken down into simpler operations until at last a level is reached at which there is no question of intelligence: A particular neuron either fires or doesn't fire, for example. Each of the successively less intelligent homunculi is eventually 'discharged' in this manner.

The most basic, unintelligent operations out of which intelligent homuncular systems emerge are supposed to be computational operations, analogous to the on-off switches in a digital computer that represent the 0s and 1s of binary code. While there is no intelligence at this most basic level, there is computation; intelligence is supposed to be a phenomenon that emerges out of computation. Computation is just rule-governed manipulation of syntactically structured symbols. The neuron firings, or whatever the most basic operations are taken to be in a particular homuncular system, are taken to be basic elements of representational states; these representational states are taken to possess intrinsically some sort of formal structure that encodes their representational content.

Homuncular functionalism shares the basic claim of functionalism: Mental states are essentially identified by their causal roles, not by any subjective element. Homuncular functionalism takes this basic claim and marries it to two other notions: First, minds are ensembles of cognitive modules that realize various intelligent capacities. Second, these modules can be broken down into progressively less intelligent modules until a level is reached at which no intelligence remains; the basic processes are purely computational.[16]

Homuncular functionalism, because it concentrates on cognitive capacities rather than on qualitative states, may not obviously seem vulnerable to the absent qualia objection and the inverted spectrum problem. Conceivably, however, a theorist might attempt to explain pain perception or color perception using a homuncular strategy. In that case, the familiar problems plaguing attempts to give functional analyses of qualitative states would arise: It does not seem, intuitively, that pain perception and color perception are defined in terms of the causal roles of internal states; pain perception and color perception are defined in terms of how they feel to the agent whose states they are.

Notice that so far, the objections discussed to various versions of functionalism have concentrated mostly on functionalism's failure to give an intuitively satisfying account of the nature of qualitative states. The reader may be wondering, What about intentional states? Might some version of functionalism provide an adequate account of intentional states, even if functionalism fails as an account of qualitative states? With this question in mind, let us turn to an objection against any version of functionalism, raised by John Searle.

AN OBJECTION TO FUNCTIONALISM:
SEARLE'S CHINESE ROOM

An intriguing argument has been advanced by John Searle, to the effect that no version of functionalism can possibly give an adequate account of intentional states (such as propositional attitudes). In order to understand Searle's argument, and to see why it has force against any version of functionalism, we must expand our discussion of functionalism to take note of the relationship between functionalism and *the computational theory of mind*. This relationship has already been suggested in our discussion of Turing machine functionalism and homuncular functionalism, but let us now make the relationship explicit.

Functionalism as a general theoretical orientation toward the mental has given rise to the computational theory of mind (or, as Searle calls it, 'strong artificial intelligence'). Once the basic claim of functionalism is accepted, that the essence of a given mental state is not its physical realization but its functional role, it becomes possible to draw an analogy between mental states and computational states, between minds and computer programs. Computers with different hardware can be in equivalent computational states, by virtue of running the same program and being at the same point in the program. Analogously, it can be conjectured that different systems (humans, silicon-based extraterrestrials, sophisticated robots) could all be in the same mental state, by virtue of being in the same functional state. The slogan 'the mind is to the brain as software is to hardware' is a pithy characterization of the computational theory of mind.

One influential version of the computational theory of mind is Jerry Fodor's 'language of thought hypothesis'.[17] According to Fodor, mental processes are operations on syntactically structured (sentencelike) internal representations; these operations take place according to rules we are 'hardwired' to follow, just as a computer is 'hard-wired' to compute in its machine language.

To believe that snow is white is, for Fodor, to have, appropriately realized in one's brain, a neural representation that means snow is white. To desire to make snowballs is to have, appropriately realized in one's brain, a neural representation of making snowballs. These two internal representations obtain their representational content by virtue of some sort of causal relationship with the things they represent.[18] The two representations could interact, purely in virtue of their intrinsic formal structure, to yield a new representation meaning that one desires to make balls out of white stuff. Searle's anti-functionalist argument is explicitly advanced against the computational theory of mind (though again, as we shall soon see, it has force against any version of functionalism). The argument is usually called 'the Chinese room argument' and it first appeared in 1980.[19]

Here is how it goes: There is a small room. The room has no windows, just two slots in the door. Inside the room is a person, call her Dagmar. Dagmar speaks only English; she can neither read nor write Chinese. Inside the room with Dagmar is a long list of peculiar strings of symbols. Dagmar also has some blank paper, and some simple instructions written in English. The instructions tell Dagmar something like the following: When a sheet with symbols on it comes through the top slot in the door, look at your list of strings of symbols. When you find a string of symbols that matches the ones that just came through the top slot, copy the immediately following line of symbols from your list onto blank paper and stick the resulting sheet out through the bottom slot in the door.

Unknown to Dagmar, the symbols are Chinese ideograms. The long list of strings of symbols possessed by Dagmar is a list of questions and appropriate answers in Chinese. When a sheet with symbols on it comes into the room through the top slot, a question in Chinese has been posed. When Dagmar finds the same string of symbols on her list and copies down the immediately following string of symbols, Dagmar is supplying an appropriate answer to the question in Chinese.

Notice how the situation would appear to someone outside the room. A question in Chinese goes in, an appropriate answer in Chinese comes out. It looks as if someone, or something, in the room understands Chinese. But Searle contends that neither Dagmar, nor the system consisting of Dagmar and her equipment, understands Chinese.

Searle's Chinese room example illustrates that a system duplicating the input/output function of a genuine understander of Chinese would not thereby understand Chinese. But Searle's argument goes deeper than this anti-behaviorist point. According to Searle, the resources utilized in the Chinese room are the only resources to which a computational theorist of mind, or any sort of functionalist, is entitled to appeal in giving an account of what it is to have an intentional state or to undergo a mental process. And Searle believes that these resources are inadequate.

According to functionalism, to believe that snow is white is just to have (appropriately realized in one's brain) a token of some neural state that plays a particular functional role. A mental process such as understanding a sentence is, for the functionalist, just the processing of structured internal representations according to physically realized rules. Any system that had the right internal representations and rule-governed processing of those representations would, thereby, possess certain propositional attitudes and be undergoing certain mental processes. In other words, the *syntax* (formal structure) of internal representations suffices to guarantee that these representations have intrinsic *semantic* or *intentional* properties (mean something to the agent whose states they are).

Dagmar, in the Chinese room, possesses a lot of representations of Chinese sentences, and she manipulates them according to rules. Computational processing of syntactically structured representations is clearly going on inside the Chinese room. It looks as if the functionalist is going to have to say that Dagmar, or the system composed of Dagmar and her list of symbols and her instructions, understands Chinese. But there is no understanding of Chinese present.

Searle convincingly makes the case that the possession and formal manipulation of symbols does not suffice for the possession of genuinely intentional states such as understanding. Semantic (intentional) properties do not necessarily emerge out of computational manipulation of syntax. Functionalism must be wrong. It leaves out the essential feature of intentional states and mental processes: Intentional states and mental processes are consciously experienced, from the subjective point of view, by selves or agents. Searle calls this latter feature of mental states their 'intrinsic intentionality'. (Intrinsic intentionality is contrasted with the derived intentionality that, for example, sentences have. A sentence means something only because conscious agents intend it to mean something. A conscious state itself, however, depends on nothing else for its representationality or aboutness.)

The Chinese room argument is similar to the absent qualia argument against functionalism in that it accuses functionalism of neglecting the essential subjective aspects of mental states. What is unique about the Chinese room argument is that it points to the subjective aspects of an intentional state—understanding Chinese sentences—rather than to the subjective aspects of a qualitative state such as pain. An argument similar to the Chinese room argument could presumably be run to show that formal symbol possession and manipulation do not suffice for the possession of any intentional states including propositional attitudes.

It is important to see that the Chinese room argument is just as forceful against Lewis's commonsense functionalism as it is against computational versions of functionalism. Specifying the functional roles of internal state types via Ramsey sentences fails to capture the subjective, first-person awareness that essentially characterizes all mental states, including propositional attitudes. In pointing to intrinsic intentionality, Searle points to the feature that ties qualitative states and propositional attitudes together as mental states; both have subjective aspects that cannot be captured in any objective, third-person specification.

Searle's Chinese room argument is often understood as a challenge to the idea that a computer or robot could ever really think merely in virtue of running some program. Searle is often taken as predicting that there will never be a conscious non-biological computer such as Hal 9000 (featured in the 1969 film *2001: A Space Odyssey*) or a conscious robot such as the character Data (of the television program "Star Trek: The Next Generation"). This is apparently a fair interpretation of Searle's view. Searle argues that we attribute consciousness to other creatures more on the basis of their having a physiology similar to ours than on the basis of their exhibiting behavior similar to ours. If a machine could think, it would be because it has the right causal powers, and, according to Searle, any actual machine that has thoughts would have to duplicate the causal powers of the brain. Searle thinks it is empirically unlikely that any machine we build out of stuff other than what we're made of would have such causal powers. Thus, even if a non-biological machine that acted like Hal or Data were built, Searle would deny that we would possess good reason to attribute consciousness to it. Searle argues that so far as we have good reason to believe, only biological creatures with a certain level of brain development possess states with intrinsic intentionality (subjectively apprehended content).[20]

DOES THE CHINESE ROOM ARGUMENT WORK?

THE SYSTEMS REPLY

It may be wondered whether Searle's Chinese room argument really is fatal to functionalism, particularly to homuncular functionalism, as an account of the nature of intentional states. After all, the homuncular functionalist is trying to give a *theory* of where intrinsic intentionality (subjective understanding) comes from. The homuncular functionalist's argument is that genuine intelligence or understanding emerges out of subcapacities that are not themselves intelligent; basic neuron firings are just 'stupid' computational processes, but complex modules orchestrated out of these firing neurons can be non-stupid. Searle might be accused of denying that there could be a theory of the nature of cognition at all, and such a denial seems obscurantist. If there is intrinsic intentionality, shouldn't we be able to explain it in terms of basic causal processes? And isn't homuncular functionalism an appropriate way to do this?

Searle has replies to such complaints. First, the Chinese room argument does have force against homuncular functionalism, according to Searle; the homuncular functionalist presumably will have to say that somehow the system consisting of Dagmar and her rules and symbols understands Chinese. Searle argues that the system does *not* understand Chinese. (The case for the idea that the system *does* understand Chinese will be discussed in the remainder of the present section.) Second, the situation is even worse for the humuncular functionalist than the Chinese room argument alone would indicate. (Searle's elaboration of these further points is the topic of the next section.)

It seems initially that Searle is obviously correct that the system as a whole (Dagmar in her room with her equipment) does not understand Chinese. How could the system composed of Dagmar, together with her paper, pencils, room, and so on, understand Chinese? The possibility that the whole system might be a Chinese-understander seems absurd. But this seemingly absurd possibility can be made to look not so absurd. Known as 'the systems reply', this possibility is often taken to be the most plausible of the many responses a proponent of functionalism might make to the Chinese room argument.

The proponent of the systems reply stresses the point that Dagmar is not the entire system; Dagmar is roughly analogous to the CPU (central processing unit) of a computational system. It is plausible that the system composed of the CPU together with memory and other components is an understander; if Dagmar could somehow *be* the whole system, instead of just the CPU, she would indeed understand Chinese.

When the proponent of the systems reply suggests that the system as a whole understands Chinese, Searle makes an ingenious move: He asks us to imagine that Dagmar *internalizes* the entire system. Dagmar memorizes all her lists of ideograms. She becomes so practiced that she can instantly write out appropriate answers when written questions in Chinese are presented to her. Dagmar has, in effect, become the entire system, not just the CPU. She is still, however, mentally looking up the characters presented to her and responding with characters from her memorized lists. According to Searle, the entire system (now within Dagmar) still fails to understand Chinese.

Can the proponent of the systems reply respond? Ned Block thinks so.[21] According to Block, the non-CPU components of the system may have been internalized by Dagmar, but they are not gone. Dagmar's memorized lists are internal non-CPU components. Dagmar herself is still just the CPU. Dagmar is a system *implementing* another system, a Chinese-understanding system. Dagmar's body houses two genuinely distinct intelligent systems, and it is unreasonable to expect the Dagmar-system to be aware of the Chinese understanding enjoyed by the other system she implements. It does not follow, however, that the other system fails to genuinely understand Chinese.

It is not easy to decide whether Block's argument is plausible. Whether the systems reply invalidates Searle's Chinese room argument is very much an open question.

SEARLE ON COMPUTATION AND THE
HOMUNCULUS PROBLEM

In addition to the Chinese room argument, Searle raises some further problems for homuncular functionalism.[22] Recall that according to homuncular functionalism, intrinsic intentionality (subjectively apprehended meaning) emerges from 'stupid' low-level computational processes, neural analogues to the on-off switches that represent 1s and 0s in a computer. It is crucial to homuncular functionalism that these basic operations are intrinsically computations; intentionality emerges out of computation. But Searle argues that according to standard definitions of computation, computation is in the eye of the beholder; just about any process can be the computation of some algorithm if an intelligent agent so interprets it, and nothing is intrinsically a computational process except an intelligent agent's *conscious* performance of computations. In order for something not possessing intrinsic intentionality to be a computational process, an intelligent agent is required to interpret the process as computational. A related point is that no arrangement of physical components intrinsically possesses syntax; whether something qualifies as a sentence depends upon whether intelligent agents choose to use it as a sentence. Not only does syntax not suffice for semantics (that's the point of the Chinese room argument), but *syntax itself is observer relative.* Even the on-off switches in a digital computer fail to be intrinsically syntactic or computational states; it takes intelligent agents, after all, to interpret these ons and offs as representing the 1s and 0s of binary code. The neurons in our brains, analogously, do not all by themselves compute algorithms; it takes an intelligent agent (a big, fat homunculus) to interpret neural firings as being computational operations.

According to Searle, homuncular functionalism fails to solve the homunculus problem because this crucial homunculus always remains in the picture to interpret what goes on in the brain as having a syntax, as being computation. Searle's anti-computationalist conclusion is that it is not appropriate to utilize the notion of computational states in giving a scientific theory of the nature of intentionality or intelligence. Searle is not denying that there could be scientific theories of cognition; such theories are quite possible and desirable, according to Searle. Scientific theories, however, properly focus on intrinsic properties, not on observer-relative properties, of the objects studied. This is because science seeks to classify in terms of causal powers, and only intrinsic properties, not observer-relative properties, have causal powers. Scientific theories of cognition must be couched in biological terms, not in computational terms, since only the biology, not the computation, is objectively there and since only biological properties, unlike syntactic properties, possess genuine causal powers.[23]

Searle's arguments on this topic have deep roots, and it would go beyond the scope of this introductory volume to examine them in detail. Here it must suffice to note that Searle has raised serious questions about the tenability of any version of functionalism, including homuncular functionalism.

A BRIEF SUMMARY AND A LOOK AHEAD

Let us summarize the discussion up to this point. We have seen that there are devastating arguments against substance dualism. Mind-body theories must be materialist (or functionalist) in order not to be hopelessly out of step with the scientific, naturalistic worldview. But we have also seen that serious objections can be raised against reductive materialist mind-body theories such as type identity theory and logical behaviorism as well as against functionalism. What happens now? What are the options if one seeks a solution to the mind-body problem?

The woods are full of reductionists and functionalists, seeking to reply to the sorts of objection I have detailed in this chapter and the preceding one.

Type identity theorists continue to insist that mental properties, if such properties are real, can be identified with physical properties. I am not very sympathetic with this line. I am inclined to think that the supervenience theorists are right; mental properties supervene on physical properties but cannot be identified with physical properties due to the essential subjective nature of mental properties. The mentalistic vocabulary that describes humans as persons with contentful states has unique connotations and purposes and cannot be replaced by a purely neurophysiological vocabulary. The reader should be aware, however, that my view is controversial.

Functionalists continue to abound, also. Probably the most popular strategy at present is a variety of functionalism that might be called 'causal representationalism'. Causal representationalism takes believing and other propositional attitudes to be relations to internal mental representations and attempts to construct a theory as to how internal representation types obtain their content, in terms of causal relations with the external world.[24]

A crude example of a causal representationalist theory might be the following: A frog's mental representation that there is a fly present has the content *that there is a fly present* because, under ideal conditions, this type of representation occurs only when a fly really is present. (Actual causal representationalist theories are more sophisticated than this, of course.)

As can readily be seen from this simple example, causal representationalist theories tend to be plagued by the so-called disjunction problem, the problem of how to account for misrepresentation. It seems that under virtually any conditions, the frog can make an error and mistake a non-fly for a fly (perhaps the non-fly is a counterfeit fly dangled by a devious scientist).

What, then, makes the frog's representation mean 'there is a fly present' rather than 'there is either a fly or a non-fly present'?

Closely related to causal representationalism is what we might call 'Darwinian representationalism'. This view, defended by Ruth Millikan,[25] suggests that a particular mental representation, such as a frog's mental representation that there is a fly present, represents a fly because it fulfills its evolutionary function (that of enabling the frog to survive and reproduce) when there is a fly present.

Both causal representationalism and Darwinian representationalism are popularly considered to be 'contenders' at present, though we will not go any more deeply into the details of such theories in this book. While neither causal representationalism nor Darwinian representationalism has been decisively refuted, there exist good grounds for doubting that either of these types of theory will ever provide a satisfactory account of mental content. Searle, for example, writes

> So far no attempt at naturalizing content has produced an explanation (analysis, reduction) of intentional content that is even remotely plausible. Consider the simplest sort of belief. For example, I believe that Flaubert was a better novelist than Balzac. Now, what would an analysis of that content, stated in terms of brute physical causation or Darwinian natural selection, without using any mental terms, look like? It should be no surprise to anyone that these attempts do not even get off the ground.[26]

Searle's remark reminds us that many of our intentional mental states concern things with which we have no direct causal contact or no causal contact at all. We have beliefs about persons long dead and states of affairs long past. We can imagine the remote future, hold beliefs about fictional entities, and desire things that don't exist. Many of our mental states, in addition to being far removed from anything with which we are in causal contact, seem to have little or no relation to our ability to survive and reproduce. Causal representationalists and Darwinian representationalists may reply that their theories can handle such mental states, given sufficient theoretical complexity, but Searle may surely be forgiven for dismissing such a response as mere hand waving.

I must admit to siding with Searle on this. Neither functionalism nor type identity theory strikes me as likely to succeed, due to the fact that subjectivity is one essential property of every mental state *qua* mental state. This feature is consistently *not captured* by physicalist and functionalist mind-body theories, and I don't see how it *could* be captured; the subjective does not reduce to the objective.

If one despairs, as I do, of any reduction of mental properties ever working out, one has two basic options: One can either adopt *eliminative materialism* or adopt some version of *non-reductive materialism*.

Eliminative materialists tend to take the reductionist/physicalist ideology very seriously; one argument for eliminative materialism contends that if no reduction of mental properties to physical properties succeeds, then mental properties do not belong in serious descriptions and explanations; mental properties must be eliminated. Eliminative materialism is evaluated in Chapters 4 and 5.

Non-reductive materialists, also called property dualists, believe that mental properties do not reduce to any other sort of property. Nevertheless, according to these theorists, mental properties cannot or should not be eliminated; mental properties can legitimately enter into serious descriptions and explanations. In Chapter 6, two influential versions of non-reductive materialism, due respectively to Donald Davidson and Daniel C. Dennett, are examined. I argue that a satisfactory version of non-reductive materialism would adopt certain features of Davidson's and Dennett's theories and reject other features of these theories.

In Chapter 7, I introduce a current controversy that bears on non-reductive materialism. This controversy concerns whether the content properties of propositional attitudes may be taken to supervene locally on brain states. *Internalists* say yes; *externalists* say no. I argue in favor of internalism, as I take it that mental properties construed as essentially subjective must supervene locally on the brain.

In Chapter 8, I discuss the problem of mental causation, the most serious problem facing non-reductive materialist mind-body theories. Chapter 9 attempts to tie up loose ends as well as summarize the discussion and articulate general conclusions.

4

Arguments for
Eliminative Materialism

ONE POSSIBLE POSITION on the mind-body problem is at first sight rather startling: eliminative materialism (EM). According to EM, mental states distinguished in terms of their propositional content (propositional attitudes such as beliefs and desires) ought to be eliminated from serious descriptions and explanations; the propositional mode of classifying internal states is a relic of an outmoded 'folk theory' of human psychology, a theory that is rapidly proving false in the face of developments in neuroscience or cognitive psychology. According to the eliminativist, it is likely that there are no propositional attitude states, nor do propositional attitude concepts have any legitimate application. (Eliminativists typically are less critical of qualitative states than of propositional attitudes, for reasons that are rather unclear.)

Versions of eliminative materialism have been defended by such philosophers as Richard Rorty,[1] Paul Feyerabend,[2] Paul Churchland,[3] and Stephen Stich.[4]

Eliminative materialists call attention to the following sort of consideration: Scientists discovered that lightning was an electrical discharge and that heat was molecular motion. In this respect, lightning and heat were reduced to entities and processes falling within the scope of physics. But compare such concepts as *witch* and *demon*. Witches and demons were once accepted as real entities that figured in the explanation of a variety of events. Nowadays, however, we regard science as having shown that the events in question have very different sorts of explanation. We regard science as having shown that demons and witches do not exist. This is very different from reducing demons and witches to other entities and processes. And this is just what an eliminativist proposes to do with mental items: show that they do not exist.

I believe that EM must ultimately be rejected. In this chapter I provide a concise yet (I hope) comprehensive summary of the arguments that have been advanced in favor of EM, and I argue that none of these arguments establishes its conclusion. In Chapter 5, I consider some arguments against EM.

Arguments advanced in favor of eliminativism fall into three basic categories.

First, there is an argument predicated upon the alleged explanatory inadequacy of commonsense propositional attitude psychology. Commonsense propositional attitude psychology, known derisively in the literature as 'folk psychology', is just the everyday practice of explaining and predicting the behavior of persons by reference to what they believe, want, hope, doubt, and so on. Since I believe that the label 'folk psychology' prejudges the issue by carrying connotations of illegitimacy, I choose to use a more clumsy but more accurate name for this practice. I shall sometimes refer to the practice as 'commonsense propositional attitude psychology'; at other times I shall abbreviate and call it 'commonsense psychology'.

Second, there is the sort of argument already mentioned that compares beliefs and desires to demons and witches. This type of argument alludes to intertheoretic reduction or the unity of science, contending that commonsense psychology is unlikely to reduce to brain science and thence to physics and is therefore likely to be eliminated as false. This is the argument wherein the assumption of the reductionist/physicalist ideology, discussed in Chapter 2, becomes explicit.

Third, there is an argument based on functionalism and its attendant computational research program in cognitive psychology. Here, it is argued that computational cognitive psychology is turning out so that it explains human behavior by reference to internal causal states that are not classified in terms of propositional content and therefore cannot be identified with the beliefs, desires, and other propositional attitudes of common sense.

All of these arguments are associated with what I shall call 'the folk-theory theory'. That is, they all seem to presuppose that commonsense propositional attitude psychology is a protoscientific empirical theory that purports to explain the nature of mental phenomena, a theory with ostensibly the same purpose as scientific psychological theories, vulnerable to disproof depending upon outcomes in empirical science. If the folk-theory theory were shown to be mistaken, the arguments for EM would all be undermined. Before I examine the arguments for EM individually, therefore, I will make some general critical observations about the folk-theory theory.

THE FOLK-THEORY THEORY

It has become popular to assert that the deliverances of common sense on any given topic are not to be given any special weight. One era's common sense is the next era's obvious falsehood. We do not know which of our current 'indubitable truths' will turn out to be doubtful after all in the light of future empirical discoveries and conceptual changes.

Consider the fact that in earlier centuries, it was common sense to explain a person's depressive temperament by saying that the person had an excess of 'black bile'. There was a prevalent belief system, one endorsed by the scientists of the day as well as by ordinary folk, according to which personality traits were determined by which of four 'humors' (one of which was called 'black bile') happened to be predominant in an individual. The theory of the four humors, however, was abandoned, and a different mode of explaining personality traits took its place. Conventional wisdom changes over time, and this makes philosophers nervous about clinging to the conventional wisdom of our own era as representing an absolute truth.

The example of the four humors raises another interesting point: Sometimes a theory can work for certain purposes without being true. In the past, when the four humors theory was accepted, a physician might have attributed the depression of his patient to an excess of black bile and prescribed exercise and sunshine, it being supposed that exercise and sunshine reduce the amount of black bile in the system. The prescribed treatment might very well work, since in some cases exercise and sunshine do alleviate depression. There is no such substance as black bile in the human body, however. Applications of the black bile theory worked in some cases, but for the wrong reasons.

Eliminative materialism in the philosophy of mind proceeds from the suspicion that commonsense psychology might be relevantly similar to the black bile theory: It might work, but for the wrong reasons. There might be no real propositional attitudes—no beliefs, desires, intentions.

Is commonsense psychology in fact relevantly similar to the black bile theory? Is commonsense psychology the sort of theory that could turn out to be false and be replaced by a very different sort of theory? This question is directly addressed in Chapter 5. In this section of the present chapter, I shall confine myself to examining critically the notion of a folk theory in more general terms.

The notion that today's commonsense 'truths' might be falsifiable 'folk theories' has become widespread. To mention just one example, it has been suggested that it is 'folk linguistics' to think sentences have meanings built up out of the meanings of the component words; 'meaning' may be a folk-theoretical term that turns out to have no legitimate application.[5] One problem with this philosophical orientation is that different theorists use the vaguely pejorative term 'folk theory' in strikingly different ways. Some descriptive/explanatory systems described as folk theories do appear to be speculative protoscience, highly vulnerable to being proven false; other systems called folk theories are disanalogous in that it is not clear what evidence, if any, would falsify them, and it is not clear that they are protoscientific attempts to describe the structure of reality. An example will be helpful here.

Proponents of the folk-theory theory are fond of talking about something called 'folk physics'. There is disagreement, however, as to what folk physics is. Patricia Churchland, in characterizing folk physics, refers to research by psychologist Michael McCloskey, seeming to indicate that naive subjects possess a relatively uniform set of expectations regarding the behavior of moving objects, expectations that contradict the experimental findings of modern physics and resemble the hypotheses of ancient Aristotelian physics.[6] McCloskey's version of folk physics does appear to embody false empirical hypotheses. It is composed of a set of expectations or hypotheses about the behavior of macroscopic objects, hypotheses disconfirmed by observation. To the extent that the observed motion of bodies contradicts the folk hypotheses, and to the extent that scientific physics can better explain and predict what is in fact observed, folk physics in McCloskey's sense is false and merits replacement—at least insofar as our aim is the description and explanation of reality.

But compare what Daniel Dennett says about folk physics:

> Folk physics is the system of savvy expectations we all have about how middle-sized physical objects in our world react to middle-sized events. If I tip over a glass of water on the dinner table, you leap out of your chair, expecting the water to spill over the side and soak through your clothes. You know better than to try to sop up the water with your fork, just as you know you can't tip over a house or push a chain. You expect a garden swing, when pushed, to swing back.[7]

Notice that Dennett's version of folk physics does not appear likely to prove false in any clearly foreseeable way. It is true that you can't push over a house. It is true that when you push a garden swing, it tends to swing back. Likewise, it does not seem that any other theory could replace Dennett's version of folk physics. Without our everyday inductive expectations regarding the behavior of ordinary physical objects, we would have difficulty doing much of anything. Could scientific physics replace what Dennett calls 'folk physics'? It does not seem likely. The purposes served by Dennett's version of folk physics appear to be more practical than theoretical; practitioners of Dennett's folk physics are trying to get around in the world, not describe its ultimate nature.

Some so-called folk frameworks are not vulnerable to disproof. I do not mean that we cannot conceive of their being false. We can, but only by imagining that the world has changed in certain fundamental ways: Laws and regularities that now hold fail to hold. Thus, folk physics (in Dennett's sense) would be falsified if water ceased to pour or be absorbed by sponges, if it could be sopped up by forks but not by napkins. Such things are imaginable, but they are not what eliminativists have in mind when they speak of a folk theory turning out false.

It is odd to call Dennett's version of folk physics a *theory* at all. What Dennett calls 'folk physics' is a kind of know-how, not normally articulated in the form of generalizations or propositional knowledge, but rather presupposed in everyday interactions with the physical environment. Other putative 'folk theories' are odd in the same way. Michael Devitt and Kim Sterelny's version of 'folk linguistics', for example, appears to be a sort of unarticulated know-how that underlies the unavoidable human activity of learning and using natural language.[8]

The fact that different theorists use 'folk theory' in such different senses suggests that the entire notion of a folk theory is ill defined. There are many different sorts of commonsense descriptive/explanatory frameworks, some vulnerable to disproof, others not. We must not assume that all so-called folk theories are in competition with science and vulnerable to being shown false or that all folk theories require scientific vindication. To draw such a sweeping conclusion is premature without a careful examination of the many different kinds of commonsense descriptive/explanatory systems that are being lumped under the term 'folk theory'.

These general reservations regarding the notion of a folk theory having been expressed, let us now examine the three types of eliminativist argument.

ARE 'FOLK' PSYCHOLOGICAL EXPLANATIONS INADEQUATE?

One argument for EM accuses commonsense psychology of being explanatorily inadequate on the grounds that it fails to explain such phenomena as sleep, dreams, mental illness, and the behavior of abnormal subjects who have suffered brain injury.[9] This is the simplest of the arguments in favor of EM, and the easiest to dispatch.

Why should we accept that commonsense psychology's purpose includes the explanation of the behavior of abnormal, damaged subjects? Perhaps commonsense psychology has a limited sphere of applicability; it applies only to normal, undamaged human beings and its purpose is limited to predicting and explaining the rational behavior of such human beings. The fact that a theory or descriptive/explanatory framework has a limited role does not establish that the theory is false or illegitimate. An analogy between commonsense psychology and computational theory is illuminating here. Computational theory provides us with explanations of the operation of normally functioning computers, but it sheds no light on the operation of machines with malfunctioning or damaged parts. It would be ridiculous to accuse computational theory of being seriously inadequate and therefore in need of elimination on these grounds.

THE ARGUMENT FROM REDUCTIONISM

The argument from reductionism for EM is much more interesting, and more challenging, than the argument charging that commonsense psychology is explanatorily inadequate. The argument from reductionism draws eliminativist conclusions from the prediction that commonsense propositional attitude psychology will fail to reduce to neuroscience and thence to physics. This argument lies at the center of a knot of complications.

Before the idea of theory reduction can be grasped, one must be clear on what philosophers have come to regard as the model of explanation in the physical sciences, the so-called *deductive-nomological model*. A deductive-nomological explanation accounts for a particular event by subsuming that event under a general law (the term 'nomological' means lawlike).

For example, suppose we wanted to explain why, on a given occasion, a magnetic field changing in the presence of a conductor generates an electric current in the conductor. We could explain this event by reference to a general law (Faraday's law of induction): A magnetic field changing in the presence of a conductor always generates an electric current in the conductor.

Such explanations are said to be deductive because they may be couched in the form of a deductive syllogism. To utilize the same example once more: Given Faraday's law of induction as our first premise, and given as our second premise the fact that a given event constitutes a magnetic field changing in the presence of a conductor, it can be deduced (it follows as a matter of logic) that an electric current will be generated in the conductor. Of course, Faraday's law of induction might be shown false by evidence, just as it might be shown false that the event at issue was in fact a magnetic field changing in the presence of a conductor. In other words, the premises of such a syllogism may not be true. But the point is, *if* the premises were true, the conclusion would follow necessarily (this is the property that defines a valid deductive argument).[10]

In defense of the idea that all true theories must eventually be reduced to physics, it is often said that the reduction of theories is an instance of deductive-nomological explanation, where what is explained is not an event, but a theory (a law or set of laws). Just as events are explained by subsumption under covering laws, so theories are explained by subsumption under (or derivation from) more basic theories.

In the general picture of science endorsed by a reductionist, physics is basic, fundamental. The intuition is that anything that happens ought to be explainable in terms of basic physics. Less basic sciences provide approximations of such explanations, approximations made necessary by reason of the complexity of the physical facts. If we were gods, able to comprehend the complexity of the physical facts, we would not need special sciences. Since we are not gods, we find it useful to have special sciences such as chemistry, biology, psychology, and sociology, each connected by 'bridge principles' to its neighboring, more basic science. (Chemistry is connected by bridge principles to physics; biology is connected by bridge principles to chemistry; psychology is connected by bridge principles to biology; sociology is connected by bridge principles to psychology, and so on.) These bridge principles connect theoretical notions in the two sciences they join, so that the less basic science may be logically derived from the more basic. The bridge principles express property identities; they tell us that properties mentioned in higher-level sciences are identifiable with (simple or disjunctive) properties mentioned in more basic sciences.

We may distinguish the following two varieties of intertheoretic reduction: (1) a very strong notion of reduction, classically described by Ernest Nagel;[11] and (2) any of various notions of reduction less stringent than Nagel's and more recent than Nagel's.[12]

Nagel's classical version of reductionism indicates that if we require true non-basic theories to be 'reducible' to physics, this means that a non-basic theory must be logically derivable from fundamental physics together with additional true premises (bridge principles) that pertain to notions whose presence in the special theory and absence in physics prevents the derivation of the former from the latter alone. Nagel's requirements on reduction are very strong in that he requires the bridge principles to satisfy the following constraint: They must *identify* important theoretical notions occurring in the special science theory with theoretical notions available in fundamental physics. Nagel is usually understood to intend that the relevant physical properties will be non-disjunctive.

In the present context, this requirement amounts to the requirement that mental properties alluded to in commonsense psychology be type-identical with simple, non-disjunctive properties alluded to in some more basic science—biology, for instance. The relevant biological properties would be identifiable with simple, non-disjunctive chemical properties, which in turn would be identifiable with simple, non-disjunctive physical properties.

Nagel's classical model of intertheoretic reduction is now generally acknowledged to be too strong to provide a plausible account of the relationship among acceptable scientific theories at different levels. This acknowledgment proceeds from several observations.

First, even in the most successful, apparently Nagel-like examples of intertheoretic reduction, such as the reduction of thermodynamics to statistical mechanics, there is a degree of multiple realization; that is, notions utilized in the reduced theory are multiply realized in different properties at the level of the reducing theory. In the case of the reduction of thermodynamics to statistical mechanics, this multiple realization takes the following form: The notion of temperature found in the reduced theory is identified with the property of mean molecular kinetic energy within the domain of gases but is identified with other physical properties in other domains, such as the domains of solids and plasmas. This phenomenon of domain-specific reduction has been observed to be the norm and not the exception.[13]

In addition, it has been observed that even in those cases where intertheoretic reduction superficially appears to conform to the Nagel model, what is derived from the reducing theory via bridge principles is not the reduced theory itself, but an approximation or 'image' thereof.[14]

There is no consensus at present as to what exactly constitutes a successful intertheoretic reduction; all one can say for certain is that a successful intertheoretic reduction may feature some degree of multiple realization and needn't provide an actual derivation of the reduced theory from the reducing theory. Whatever a successful intertheoretic reduction may be, EM predicts that commonsense psychology will not enjoy such a relationship with physical science, and this failure of reducibility is taken to indicate that propositional attitude properties are not worthy of serious scientific consideration. Basically, the proponent of the argument from reductionism is predicting that mature science will not mention propositional attitudes in its theories, nor will these theories mention anything identifiable with propositional attitudes.

THE REDUCTIONIST/PHYSICALIST IDEOLOGY
IS SELF-DEFEATING

In Chapter 2 I spoke of a certain reductionist/physicalist ideology, characterized by allegiance to the idea that all legitimate descriptive/explanatory concepts must ultimately correspond to physical properties. Adherence to such an ideology obviously underlies the eliminativist's demand that commonsense propositional attitude psychology must either reduce or be eliminated. My case against the argument from reductionism for EM will take the following form: I will attempt to show that the reductionist/physicalist ideology cannot coherently be endorsed by theorists who take themselves to be agents. This is because propositional attitude properties *must* be recognized, by those who take themselves to be agents, as entering into legitimate causal explanations of action. Since the possibility (indeed, the strong probability) exists that propositional attitude properties may not be reducible to physical properties, theorists run the risk of defeating themselves by denying their own agency if they endorse the reductionist/physicalist ideology (hereafter, RPI).

Explanations of action making reference to propositional attitudes are plausibly taken to be legitimate causal explanations.[15] RPI demands that properties entering relevantly into legitimate causal explanations must reduce to physical properties; if not, they must be eliminated. Suppose propositional attitude properties turn out not to reduce to physical properties (as the eliminativist himself predicts). Suppose, accordingly, that we eliminate propositional attitude properties and their associated causal explanations. This would amount to eliminating agency from the world, since agents are precisely persons who act for reasons (persons whose behavior is causally explained in propositional attitude terms). Even an eliminativist presumably does not want to deny that he is an agent. Thus, the eliminativist who is inclined to endorse RPI is faced with a dilemma: Propositional attitude properties must either reduce to physical properties or he himself is not an agent.

I have argued in previous chapters that there is good reason to believe that propositional attitude properties won't reduce to physical properties, though my argument stressed subjectivity rather than stressing the unlikelihood that mature science will explicitly recognize propositional attitudes. It is plausible that mental properties supervene on physical properties rather than reducing to physical properties. Mental properties, though realized in physical properties, are essentially subjective, and so cannot be identified with objective, physical properties. But we cannot eliminate mental properties on grounds of their failure to be reducible; we cannot eliminate mental properties because to eliminate mental properties would mean eliminating our very *selves*. (The contention that EM is a self-defeating position is probably the most powerful argument against EM, and it is elaborated further in Chapter 5.)

THE ARGUMENT FROM FUNCTIONALISM

There is another argument in favor of eliminative materialism that appeals not to physicalistic reductionism but to the computer-inspired research program in cognitive science. I call this argument 'the argument from functionalism' because the computational research program in cognitive science is an extension of the basic functionalist idea that mental properties are functional properties. The argument from functionalism for EM has been advanced by Stephen Stich.[16]

Stich's chief complaint about commonsense psychology is that it individuates (types) internal causal states by means of propositions, ascribed by the that-clauses of ordinary language. Stich joins many other philosophers in contending that propositional individuation of state types is not very accurate in capturing the causal roles of internal state types. The best theory of our true cognitive organization, Stich believes, must individuate internal states according to their causal powers, and such causal powers could be more accurately indexed by syntactic descriptions than by propositions.

The words 'syntax' and 'syntactic', though commonly used by philosophers these days, are troublesome. It is often not clear what a given theorist means by them. I will use 'syntactic', as I take Stich to be using it, to mean pertaining to the arrangement of the components of some meaningful inscription. Syntactic features of states and inscriptions are to be contrasted with semantic features. The latter have to do with meaning and reference; the former have to do with arrangement of components.

In order to understand Stich's contention that propositional individuation of internal state types is inaccurate in capturing the causal roles of internal state types, consider the following. Hilary Putnam and Tyler Burge have argued that different propositional contents may appropriately be ascribed to persons who are in exactly the same internal causal/functional state, merely because these persons are embedded in different physical environments or linguistic communities.[17]

I believe that this position, which might be called 'externalism' with regard to mental content, is confused in significant ways; I will make my objections clear in Chapter 7. Rather than discuss content externalism in detail here, let us simply note that if content externalism is true, the that-clauses we use to characterize the content of propositional attitudes are more attuned to capturing a person's relations to his or her environment than to capturing the causal roles of the person's internal states.

Putnam has also argued that persons in different internal causal/functional states can appropriately be described as being in states with the same propositional content.[18] This is another way of making the point that propositional content, as ascribed by that-clauses, is a clumsy device for capturing the causal roles of internal states. It is worthwhile to quote Putnam at some length on this topic:

> ... not only is it false that different humans are in one and the same computational state whenever they believe that there are a lot of cats in the neighborhood, or whatever, but members of different physically possible species who are sufficiently similar in their linguistic behavior in a range of environments to permit us to translate some of their utterances as meaning, 'there are a lot of cats in the neighborhood,' or whatever, may have computational states that lie in an incomparable 'space' of computational states. ... The idea that there is *one* computational state that every being who believes that there are a lot of cats in the neighborhood (or whatever) *must* be in is false.[19]

Stich uses his own examples to make these points and argues that assigning content to internal states is a confused and inaccurate way to index the causal roles of those states. If we want to individuate mental states by their causal powers (and this is what cognitive psychology presumably wants to do), then we would do better to describe mental states in terms of properties that clearly have causal relevance, such as physical properties or (as Stich claims) syntactic properties.

RESPONSES TO THE ARGUMENT FROM FUNCTIONALISM

Suppose that the scenario envisioned by Stich has come to pass. Suppose that cognitive science has matured and has turned out to explain cognition by means of reference to states that bear no great resemblance in causal role to the beliefs and desires of common sense in that these states are not individuated by propositional content but by syntax or physical form. Cognitive theories would resemble uninterpreted computer programs. Would such a turn of events establish the conclusion that there really are no beliefs and desires, that commonsense propositional attitude psychology is a false theory?

It would, so long as it was initially accepted that commonsense mental concepts must be taken seriously by cognitive science in order to be legitimate. While it is debatable whether all legitimate causal-explanatory notions must explicitly be vindicated by inclusion in scientific theories,[20] there is a way to respond to Stich's argument for EM that does not require us to deny that legitimate causal-explanatory notions must be vindicated by inclusion in scientific theories.

One can argue as follows: It is not going to turn out that cognitive science recognizes no states significantly akin to the beliefs and desires of commonsense psychology. Such an outcome, if not outright conceptually inconceivable, is so unlikely that its possibility may be safely ignored. It is built into the very notion of cognition that cognitive beings possess propositional attitude states, of approximately the commonsense sort. Hence, if you have anything worthy of being called *cognitive* science, you have propositional attitudes. If Stich believes that cognitive science is going to end up purely syntactic, then what he really believes is that cognition itself will eventually be eliminated from the book of scientifically legitimate concepts. (Perhaps he should have called his 1983 book *From Folk Psychology to Non-Cognitive Science.*)

Terence Horgan and James Woodward have made a relevant point in this context. While Stich may be correct that cognitive science may for some purposes deal with states not described as possessing propositional content, these non-contentful states may be parts of larger, more complex states ('gerrymandered' from the point of view of certain concerns of cognitive science, but real states nonetheless). These larger states may correctly be identified as propositional attitudes, even if their simpler component states cannot. These propositional attitude states may legitimately be seen as being causes, though perhaps not 'minimal causes', of behavior.[21] To Horgan and Woodward's point I would add the following: Even when cognitive science deals with non-contentful components of the complex states that are propositional attitudes, cognitive science must implicitly recognize the existence of these larger, complex, contentful states, on pain of not being *cognitive* science at all.

I am deliberately stressing the point that the concept of cognition essentially involves the existence of propositional attitude states and that cognitive science cannot eliminate the concept of cognition without destroying its own subject matter. With this (provocative, I hope) suggestion in mind, let us turn to arguments against eliminative materialism.

5

Arguments Against
Eliminative Materialism

IN THE PREVIOUS CHAPTER I attacked eliminative materialism (EM), the view that beliefs, desires, and other states that enter into commonsense psychological explanations might be fictions, by undermining arguments that have been advanced in favor of EM. In the present chapter I will concentrate on considerations against EM. These considerations against eliminativism consist of two closely related arguments: the argument that commonsense psychology could not conceivably prove false[1] and the argument that EM is self-defeating or self-refuting. Taken together, these form what we might call (with apologies to Kant) a transcendental deduction[2] of the propositional attitudes.

COULD COMMONSENSE PSYCHOLOGY
CONCEIVABLY PROVE FALSE?

Jerry Fodor has expressed very nicely the spirit behind the argument that commonsense propositional attitude psychology could not conceivably prove false:

> Even if [commonsense psychology] were dispensable *in principle,* that would be no argument for dispensing with it. ... What's relevant to whether commonsense psychology is worth defending is its dispensability *in fact.* And here the situation is absolutely clear. We have no idea of how to explain ourselves to ourselves except in a vocabulary which is *saturated* with belief/desire psychology. One is tempted to transcendental argument: What Kant said to Hume about physical objects holds, mutatis mutandis, for the propositional attitudes; we can't give them up *because we don't know how to.*[3]

Indeed, there is something odd and paradoxical about the idea that commonsense propositional attitude psychology could prove false (at least, such an idea would appear very odd to the person in the street, whose intuitions regarding commonsense concepts were unpolluted by exposure to philosophical theories). What evidence can we imagine that would show commonsense psychology to be false? What could conceivably establish the non-existence of propositional attitudes?

Recall that we are taking commonsense psychology to be not only an explanatory and predictive calculus, but also the conceptual framework or descriptive vocabulary in terms of which humans are seen as rational beings (cognizers). Notice that I am using the term 'rational' in a particular sense; by 'rational being' I mean only *a being that does things for reasons*. There is another sense of 'rational' that is contrasted with 'irrational', but that is not my intended sense. As I use the term, 'rational' is contrasted with 'non-rational'. Whether commonsense psychology could conceivably prove false is, given this use of the word 'rational', the question of *whether it could conceivably turn out that humans are not cognitive creatures after all*.

It may seem that humans are just obviously cognitive creatures (rational beings in my stipulated sense of 'rational'), that this is a truth too fundamental to be seriously questioned; to question it would be to lose what Bertrand Russell described as "that feeling for reality which ought to be preserved even in the most abstract studies."[4] Yet, we must acknowledge that to an eliminativist, it seems obvious that *any* theoretical framework could prove false.

According to an eliminativist, it could very well turn out that there were no such phenomena as rationality and cognition. The eliminativist claims that those terms derive their meanings from a theory that may be a thoroughly false description of reality. How does one reply to an eliminativist?

It is worth bringing out in this discussion that to characterize our concepts of beliefs, and the like, as theoretical concepts is already to beg a question, namely, whether we know directly that we have beliefs and other sorts of mental state. If we do have such direct knowledge, then beliefs, etc., are not for us theoretical entities. For them to be theoretical entities, we would have to infer their existence from some evidence we had that was epistemically prior to their postulation.

I believe we do have direct, non-inferential knowledge of our own propositional attitudes. We are introspectively acquainted with the contents of our own beliefs and desires. Introspection is currently out of fashion in philosophy, but I will be bold: I take it that Descartes had a point when he observed that he could not be deceived as to the existence of his own thoughts.

Of course, Descartes did not have in mind such phenomena as repressed or unconscious thoughts, but he seems wholly correct so long as we confine ourselves to the realm of ordinary introspection: We introspect *something*, and part of what we introspect is appropriately called 'belief'.

Granted, the term 'belief' is sometimes used to refer to unconscious or merely dispositional states, with which we are not directly acquainted (at least, not until some stimulus calls these states to consciousness). For example, I might be told that I unconsciously believe that my father hates me and not realize this until a hypnotherapist causes me to acknowledge it; I might be inclined to assent to the proposition that Buckingham Palace is not filled with pickles,[5] but this belief might never have crossed my mind until somebody mentioned it to me. The use of the term 'belief' to refer to such unconscious and dispositional states may be legitimate, but it is (I would argue) derived from the more basic use of the term 'belief' to refer to states with which believers have direct acquaintance.

The fact that we are directly acquainted with our own beliefs indicates that beliefs exist. We may be certain of the existence of *phenomena* with which we are epistemically acquainted, and we may justifiably believe that these introspected phenomena have some physiological basis or other. When I say to myself, "By 'belief' I mean *that*," performing an act of inner ostension, I refer directly to an introspected phenomenon, the existence of which is beyond doubt; less directly, I refer to whatever turns out to be responsible for that introspected phenomenon, presumably a physical state of my brain.

By saying that beliefs are introspectible states, that we are directly acquainted with our beliefs, I mean only that we have a unique introspective awareness of our own conscious thoughts. I do not mean to imply that beliefs in general possess any qualitative 'feel' such as a pain, or a scent, or a view of the Grand Canyon (though sensory beliefs about one's immediate environment may be said to have qualitative content). Many beliefs are purely cognitive and have no qualitative dimension at all. Nevertheless, that we do have beliefs, whose contents can be more or less accurately captured by means of propositional that-clauses, is subjectively evident. If someone asks me if I believe that Stephen Schiffer wears colorful socks, I can immediately give a truthful reply, by means of consulting what I know immediately.

There are those who ridicule such pronouncements regarding the certainty of introspective knowledge. Paul Churchland, for example, comments:

> ... an introspective judgment is just an instance of an acquired habit of conceptual response to one's internal states, and the integrity of any particular response is always contingent on the integrity of the acquired conceptual framework (theory) in which the response is framed. Accordingly, one's *introspective* certainty that one's mind is the seat of beliefs and desires may be as badly misplaced as was the classical man's *visual* certainty that the star-flecked sphere of the heavens turned daily.[6]

Is Churchland correct that we must interpret our introspected states in accordance with some learned conceptual framework that might prove false? On one reading of Churchland's suggestion, the idea is that we get some data and then infer from the data that we have beliefs and the like. There is an innocent point here, and one not so innocent. The innocent point is that anything we know involves some belief, and to have a belief one must have concepts. So if we know by introspection what our own mental states are, we must have the concepts that are involved in the beliefs that constitute our knowledge. But it does not follow from this, as Churchland sometimes seems to think, that it is epistemically possible that every belief be false, simply in virtue of beliefs' involving concepts.

I wish to make clear where I agree with Churchland and where I disagree with him. I agree with him that pronouncements of certainty regarding the truth of what is introspectively experienced must be regarded with extreme caution. For example, suppose I am perusing the literature on free will and determinism, and I find a certain theorist claiming that he is just certain, for introspective reasons, that he is a free 'agent self' who can escape the causal nexus and make free choices to perform morally significant acts. This is a claim to which I would not attach much weight. People can surely claim to be certain introspectively of all sorts of false claims. In addition, psychological experiments would seem to indicate that we do not have reliable introspective access to such matters as whether certain information has influenced our behavior.[7] I do not doubt the implications of such data; it seems clear that the *content* of introspection is deeply colored by theory and prejudice. What I do doubt is that our certainty of the *existence* of introspection itself is the product of a theory.

That we introspect could not conceivably be false, even if beliefs we form on the basis of introspection are often false. To say that we introspect the existence of beliefs and desires is just to say that we introspect states whose contents may appropriately be characterized by means of that-clauses. I would argue that no scientific evidence can be imagined that would show either that we do not introspect our own internal states or that it is illegitimate to describe these internal states as possessing propositional content.

I also take issue with Churchland's comparison of the introspective certainty of the existence of beliefs with the purported ancient 'certainty' that the spheres of the heavens moved. Nobody ever enjoyed introspective acquaintance with the heavenly spheres. Ancient persons who subscribed to the celestial sphere theory could be certain of no more than that they perceived a certain apparent motion: It looked as if the heavens were revolving. The heavenly spheres were posited as an explanatory hypothesis to account for the observed apparent motion. Perhaps in the heyday of the theory, many did not think to question it, but still, when a better theory was propounded, one that did not feature celestial spheres, most people eventually accepted it. Moreover, even during the period when the celestial sphere theory was widely accepted, there were other theories available. Some ancient Greek philosophers thought the earth moved rather than the stars and planets; so, it could not have been inconceivable that the motion of the stars and planets was only apparent.

It may help here to emphasize that there seems to be nothing that plays the role of evidence about our own mental states that we could cite as what we go on when challenged to justify our beliefs about conscious mental states. This is one way of bringing out the disanalogy with beliefs in heavenly spheres, where clearly the ancients could have pointed to their evidence. In the case of beliefs, we are introspectively acquainted with the items whose existence is at issue. And it is for precisely this reason that no theory purporting to establish the non-existence of these items is apt to win wide acceptance.

A remark by Patricia Churchland illustrates more strongly than any other passage in the literature the radical nature of some eliminative materialists' construal of commonsense psychological concepts: " ... it is possible that the folk theory that gives 'awareness' its meaning might turn out to be displaced by a superior theory. Accordingly, just as it turned out that there was no such thing as impetus, there may be no such thing as awareness."[8]

How could it turn out that there was no such thing as awareness? Does Churchland mean to imply that in the golden age of neuroscience we will all be unconscious? Our own consciousness, again, is something with which we are directly acquainted. No discovery made by science is likely to convince us of the non-existence of consciousness. Any discovery made by science as to the physiological grounds of awareness will be an addition to our consciousness, not a replacement of it. The ordinary concept of awareness is not the construct of a theory. Here I cannot resist quoting Colin McGinn, who has remarked, in a review of the book from which the preceding quotation was taken:

> When Descartes asserted that he could not be wrong in supposing himself to be a thinking being he was not being misled by his ignorance of neuroscience. Tell him all the neuroscience there is to know, and he will not be justified in concluding, "Oh, so I'm not really thinking after all." At any rate, it is this kind of intuitive conviction that Churchland needs to undermine—and no amount of tired rhetoric about the intellectual conservativeness of philosophers is going to turn the trick.[9]

I have been arguing that it is just evident, that it could not conceivably be false, that people have propositional attitude states. No evidence adduced by neuroscience, or any other science, can be imagined that would convince ordinary users of propositional attitude concepts that those concepts failed to be exemplified.

In this context it is useful to note the following: Some philosophers have suggested that eliminable concepts always contain some aspect that turns out, on empirical grounds, not to be exemplified by anything in the physical world. Eliminativists like to compare propositional attitudes to demons. Both, they suggest, have served to explain aspects of human behavior. The concept of a demon, however, is the concept of an agency exorcisable by means of certain rituals. Events of alleged demon possession may be tested to see if exorcism rites ever alleviate the condition. Propositional attitude notions are not like this. Every aspect of propositional attitude concepts is exemplified by intimately familiar subjective states, and no empirical test of which we can conceive would show that propositional attitude concepts failed to be exemplified.[10]

Compare the notion of Santa Claus. Does the notion of Santa Claus reduce to the notion of benevolent, gift-giving parents who fill the Christmas stockings after the children have gone to bed? Or is the notion of Santa Claus properly eliminated from serious descriptions and explanations because Santa Claus does not exist? The latter, presumably; while part of the functional role definitive of Santa Claus is fulfilled by benevolent parents, the notion of Santa Claus also contains elements that no plausible candidate satisfies, such as living at the North Pole, coming down the chimney, flying in a sleigh pulled by reindeer, and so on. I challenge readers to find some element inherent in the notion of a propositional attitude that similarly fails to be satisfied by anything in reality. Propositional attitudes simply are not relevantly similar to demons and Santa Claus.

IS ELIMINATIVE MATERIALISM SELF-DEFEATING?

The argument that EM is self-defeating or self-refuting may be formulated (in loose, intuitive terms) in the following manner: It is a consequence of EM that there are no propositional attitudes. But to accept EM, or to assert EM's truth, inescapably involves taking an attitude toward a proposition. Therefore, in the very act of endorsing or asserting EM, one proves that EM cannot be correct.

Paul Churchland lampoons the argument that eliminativism is self-defeating by comparing it to a fictional argument supposedly advanced by a vitalist against an anti-vitalist. The vitalist hopes to prove to the anti-vitalist that anti-vitalism is self-defeating. The vitalist argues as follows:

> The anti-vitalist says that there is no such thing as vital spirit. But this claim is self-refuting. The speaker can expect to be taken seriously only if his claim cannot. For if the claim is true, then the speaker does not have vital spirit and must be *dead*. But if he is dead, then his statement is a meaningless string of noises, devoid of reason and truth.[11]

Lynne Rudder Baker has pointed out that this bit of satire does not seriously undermine the argument that eliminativism is self-defeating.[12] As Baker notes, it is possible to reply to Churchland as follows: The vitalist's argument simply is not parallel to the anti-eliminativist's argument. The vitalist is clearly begging the question against the anti-vitalist by assuming that vital spirit is necessary in order to be alive. It is a perfectly conceivable possibility that vital spirit is *not* necessary in order to be alive, which is what makes the vitalist's assumption illegitimate. If vitalism is false, it does not necessarily follow that everyone is dead; there are other possibilities to be entertained. The case of propositional attitudes is notably different. The anti-eliminativist may appear to be assuming illegitimately that propositional attitudes must exist in order for it to be possible to make meaningful claims, but the assumption here is legitimate due to the lack of any conceivable alternative. The lack of such an alternative is the very thing that the anti-eliminativist is trying to point out. It was not incoherent to suppose that vitalism might be false; even when vitalism was a popular theory, it was conceivable that some other account of the nature of life might turn out to be correct. But it is incoherent to suppose that there might not be propositional attitudes. In the very act of stating the supposition, one refutes the supposition.

Baker distinguishes three ways in which EM appears to be self-defeating.

First, anyone who *accepts* that EM is rationally acceptable lapses into pragmatic incoherence because EM undermines the concept of rational acceptability. That is, the notions of *accepting a theory* and of *having good reason to accept a theory* are both part and parcel of commonsense psychology, which EM seeks to eliminate.

Second, anyone who *asserts* EM lapses into pragmatic incoherence because EM undermines the concept of assertion. How can there be assertion without belief?

The latter may require some elucidation. My asserting that snow is white—as opposed to my merely mouthing the words— requires that I have certain beliefs or intentions. Asserting that P, unlike saying that P, is what philosophers sometimes call a *speech act*; one cannot assert P accidentally, as one can accidentally say something one didn't intend. There is an amusing example that illustrates the difference between saying that and asserting that.

President John F. Kennedy once made a speech in Germany in which he uttered the phrase, 'Ich bin ein Berliner'. What Kennedy intended to express was 'I am a citizen of Berlin'; he wanted to express solidarity with the people of Berlin. But, it was a gaffe for Kennedy to say 'ein Berliner' rather than just 'Berliner'. The use of 'ein' in combination with 'Berliner' colloquially indicates that what is meant by 'Berliner' in the context is not a citizen of Berlin, but a sugary pastry similar to a jelly roll.[13] So, in a sense, Kennedy said that he was a jelly roll. Kennedy accidentally said something he didn't intend. But it wouldn't be correct to say that Kennedy *asserted* that he was a jelly roll. In order for Kennedy to make an assertion with that content, he would have had to believe, or intend to communicate, the proposition that he was a jelly roll. And, of course, Kennedy had no such belief or intention.

Baker is quite right to point out that one cannot assert that EM is true without having certain beliefs or intentions regarding EM, and this is pragmatically incoherent given that EM is the idea that there are no beliefs and intentions.

Third, anyone who claims that EM is *true* lapses into pragmatic incoherence, because the notions of truth and falsity are part and parcel of commonsense psychology, the very conceptual scheme EM seeks to overthrow. (Truth and falsity are properties of propositions, and the notion of a proposition or content is a central commonsense-psychological notion.) Baker points out that we can formulate a thesis if and only if we can specify what would make it true; since EM casts suspicion on the notion of truth, EM has not even been shown to be formulable.

Hilary Putnam has advanced a version of the latter argument that deserves brief independent consideration.[14] Putnam calls attention to the reductionism implicit in EM, interpreted by Putnam as the idea that any concept worthy of being taken seriously in science must be reducible to naturalistic (physical or functional) terms. Intensional notions such as that of meaning or propositional content have been the primary target of eliminativists, but Putnam argues that notions relating to extensional semantics, such as reference and truth, are equally irreducible to naturalistic terms.[15] According to the eliminativists' own central principle, such irreducible concepts belong to 'folk theory' and have no proper place in a description of reality. Yet, as Putnam points out, the eliminativists' own most favored descriptions of reality, those given by empirical sciences such as neurobiology and computational cognitive psychology, are supposed to be *true* in the ordinary sense of truth and are supposed to *refer* to objective, mind-independent reality; this is the very essence of the eliminativists' basic philosophical orientation, scientific realism. Putnam thus nets the eliminativists in a powerful charge of inconsistency: The eliminativists themselves must utilize the very notions they wish to eliminate.

Churchland finds such arguments unconvincing; he maintains that the current pragmatic incoherence of EM is not worrisome, on the grounds that we may anticipate a new conceptual scheme that will render the entire conversation meaningless. Within this new conceptual scheme, we will have no need to utilize the concepts of propositional attitude, rational acceptability, assertion, and truth. New concepts, currently unimaginable, will replace these. What is inconceivable to us at present is not necessarily *logically impossible*.

It is not entirely innocent and uncontroversial to maintain that what is inconceivable may yet be logically possible. Even if we grant this to Churchland, however, his reply to the argument that EM is self-defeating is unimpressive. If eliminativism is, in the end, just the claim that our current conceptual scheme, involving commonsense psychological notions, may someday be overthrown, why should we care about eliminativism? It remains the case that eliminativism cannot consistently be held or asserted within the current conceptual scheme, that what eliminativism's truth would consist in is utterly inconceivable at present. It thus remains open to the opponent of eliminativism to argue that the mere possibility of a conceptual revolution gives us no reason to doubt the legitimacy of concepts that currently serve purposes no other currently imaginable concepts could serve.

Putnam agrees with this evaluation. He writes:

> [the eliminativist] has now taken on a positive program, the program of developing what Churchland called a 'successor concept to the notion of truth' and of showing that we can account for our linguistic and scientific practice (including the use of classical logic) in terms of this successor concept. I would only say that until this program is more than a gleam in the eyes of some scientific realists, I do not myself expect it to succeed. ... To me it seems that what we shall have to give up is the demand that all notions that we take seriously be reducible to the vocabulary and the conceptual apparatus of the exact sciences. I believe it is reductionism that is in trouble—not intentionality itself.[16]

Recall that there are two major arguments for EM, the argument from reductionism and the argument from functionalism (see Chapter 4). If we concentrate for a moment on the argument from functionalism as advanced by Stephen Stich,[17] we can see that there is an additional way to argue that EM is self-defeating.

Stich maintains that cognitive science is turning out such that it recognizes no states with propositional content; this, according to Stich, is reason to believe that the conceptual scheme of commonsense psychology is ripe for elimination. Stich sees no problem with a purely syntactic, wholly non-semantic theory of cognition. Within such a theory, causally relevant internal states of organisms would be described according to the arrangement of their components (syntax) and would not be interpreted as having meaning (content). It is possible to argue, however, that unless we identify some internal states of the organism as propositional attitude states, the behavior to be explained is no longer the cognitive (rational) behavior we have acknowledged it to be. (This point was made in the previous chapter, but I believe it is worthy of the following expansion.)

In the literature there is an argument for the idea that when rational behavior is the phenomenon to be explained it is necessary to have propositional attitudes in the explanation; Zenon Pylyshyn, for one, has stated a version of it.[18] Let us examine a careful reconstruction of this type of argument.[19]

The first premise is that rational behavior is stimulus-independent. An act is stimulus-independent if and only if it is not stimulus-bound. That is, an act is stimulus-independent if it can be the result of any number of different stimuli; it is not a tropistic response, nor is it a conditioned response, to some one particular stimulus. To use an example due to Pylyshyn, suppose a person (call her Pat) has come running out of a burning building. Assuming that all parties have agreed to see Pat as a cognizer, and to view her running out of the burning building as a rational act, it must be admitted that her action might have resulted from a variety of different stimuli. She might have smelled smoke. She might have heard an alarm. She might have seen flames. She might have heard Carlos yell, "Help, fire!" And so on. All rational actions are relevantly similar. More than one possible stimulus might have the same meaning or import for the rational actor, and hence, more than one stimulus might produce the same action. A rational act is a response to the meaning of a stimulus, not to the stimulus itself.

The second premise is that cognizers, by definition, act because of internal states; the causes of intelligent action are internal. This is a consequence of the inadequacy of behaviorism[20] to account for cognitive phenomena. We must postulate the existence of causally relevant internal states of rational organisms or we cannot account adequately for their complex and purposeful behavior.

Third premise: In order for some action, such as running out of a burning building, to be an appropriate (rational) response to some stimulus or other, the stimulus must mean something to the cognizer, and this meaning must interact appropriately with the cognizer's internal physical states in order to produce the appropriate behavior.

Fourth premise: A 'meaning' can have no effect on a physical organism unless that meaning is itself encoded (realized) in some physical state of the organism.

Conclusion: Therefore, some physical states of cognizers must encode the meanings of stimuli and must therefore appropriately be described as possessing propositional content.

If this argument is sound, it establishes that it is incoherent for an eliminativist to claim that admittedly cognitive or rational acts can be explained by reference to states given purely syntactic descriptions. This argument, if sound, gives us further grounds for concluding that eliminativism is a self-defeating position. If one accepts that rational actions are the things to be explained, one is stuck with propositional attitudes in the explanations.

To see the force of the argument, consider again the example of Pat in the burning building. Suppose that Pat has encountered any one of the myriad stimuli that might mean 'the building is on fire'. Now suppose that something occurs in Pat's head, and Pat subsequently runs out of the building. How do we manage to construe Pat's running out of the building as a rational or cogent response to whatever stimulus she encountered? That is, how do we see Pat's behavior as cognitive or intelligent? Surely it is no help to be given a neurophysical description of what went on in Pat's head. The fact that a system 'outputs' an uninterpreted string of symbols subsequent to being exposed to some stimulus and prior to performing some act points to no rationality connection between the act and the stimulus. What is essential to seeing the rationality connection is seeing whatever occurs in the head as symbolic, as having an interpretation, as meaning something.[21]

RETROSPECTIVE AND PREVIEW

In Chapter 4 and in the present chapter, I argued that eliminative materialism is self-defeating or self-refuting in several significantly different senses. In earlier chapters, I argued that mental properties cannot be identified with (reduced to) physical or functional properties, due to the essential subjective aspects of mental properties.

Readers may now appreciate the following situation: If we want to give a philosophical account of the nature of mental properties, we will have to do so without recourse to reduction. Several philosophers have pursued this course. I call such theories versions of *non-reductive materialism;* such theories are also called *property dualist* theories. Let us now examine two influential versions of non-reductive materialism.

❧ 6 ❧

Two Versions of
Non-Reductive Materialism

DAVIDSON: ANOMALOUS MONISM

The first version of non-reductive materialism we will discuss is that defended by Donald Davidson. He calls his position 'anomalous monism', and it has been extremely influential. Anomalous monism and its companion supervenience thesis are set out in Davidson's notoriously difficult paper, "Mental Events."[1] What follows is a (simplified) critical exposition of that paper.

Davidson begins with two 'undeniable facts':

1. Mental events are causally dependent (that is, they are caused).
2. Mental events are anomalous—they cannot be predicted and explained on the basis of physical theory (on the basis of strict laws).

Davidson's central issue is, How can both of these truths obtain? Davidson illustrates the issue by suggesting that the reader paraphrase Kant as follows. (In the paraphrased passage, Kant is talking about the anomalous character of free will vis-à-vis physical determinism. Davidson asks his readers to substitute 'anomaly' for Kant's 'freedom' and 'mental events' for Kant's 'human actions'.)

> It is as impossible for the subtlest philosophy as for the commonest reasoning to argue the anomaly [of mental events] away. Philosophy must therefore assume that no true contradiction will be found between anomaly and natural necessity in the same mental events, for it cannot give up the idea of nature any more than that of anomaly. Hence even if we should never be able to conceive how anomaly is possible, at least this apparent contradiction must be convincingly eradicated. For if the thought of anomaly contradicts itself or nature ... it would have to be surrendered in competition with natural necessity.[2]

Before we begin to explore Davidson's views on this issue, some background on Davidson's more general philosophical views will be helpful.[3]

First, what does Davidson mean by a 'mental event'? Events, for Davidson, are particular things that occupy a region of space-time; events are much like physical objects. In Davidson's words: "Events are taken to be unrepeatable, dated individuals such as the particular eruption of a volcano, the (first) birth or death of a person, the playing of the 1968 World Series, or the historic utterance of the words, 'You may fire when ready, Gridley.'"[4] Mental events are just events that can be picked out using mentalistic descriptions—descriptions featuring terms such as 'intends', 'believes', and so on, which create intensional contexts. Thus, any event that can correctly be described as a propositional attitude is, for Davidson, a mental event.

Second, why is Davidson convinced that mental events are anomalous—that they cannot be predicted and explained on the basis of strict physical laws?

To answer this question we must remind ourselves of what Davidson means by 'strict' law. A strict law, while it may possibly be statistical as opposed to deterministic, is exceptionless and universal. Davidson believes that the only strict laws are those of physics; all other scientific laws are non-strict, that is, they hold only 'other things being equal'. (Such non-strict laws are often referred to by philosophers as *ceteris paribus*—'other things being equal'—laws. The presence of a *ceteris paribus* clause in a law just means that the law is not exceptionless; there are circumstances in which the law does not hold.) Davidson sometimes seems to think that non-strict laws are not really genuine laws at all (though, as we shall see, his remarks on this topic are somewhat inconsistent).

Davidson is convinced that mental events cannot be predicted and explained on the basis of strict laws for the following reason: According to Davidson, the question 'What mental events are occurring in x's mind?' can be answered only by appeal to *holistic* and *normative* principles. Davidson believes that holism and normativity are incompatible with predictability on the basis of strict physical law.

What are holism and normativity? Holism is the following idea: The character of a propositional attitude—my believing that Albuquerque is hot in August—depends for its character on relations it bears to endless other propositional attitudes—my believing that Albuquerque is in New Mexico, that New Mexico is a state—and these owe their character to other attitudes. As a result, I am prepared to ascribe a particular attitude to you only if I am prepared to ascribe many other attitudes to you as well. We cannot ascribe attitudes one at a time.

Normativity is perhaps a more difficult idea to grasp. Normativity is essentially expressed by the words 'ought' and 'should'. There are both moral norms (rules telling us what we ought to do) and epistemic norms (rules telling us what we ought to believe). Normativity, as applied to propositional attitude ascription, includes the following idea: What propositional attitudes a person, x, really has is determined by what propositional attitudes it would be *reasonable* for an interpreter to ascribe to x on the assumption that x, like the interpreter, is rational and is largely in agreement with the interpreter. Davidson holds that within limits a person really has the propositional attitudes that he or she *ought* to have (in the epistemic sense of 'ought') given the assumptions of mutual rationality and a large base of agreement between interpreter and interpretee.

This does not rule out irrational belief; it merely constrains the ascription of irrational belief. Roughly: You are entitled to ascribe an irrational belief to me only if your so doing would result in making me more rational overall.

It seems that if mental events could be predicted and explained on the basis of physical law, the attribution of propositional attitudes could be done without recourse to holism and normativity. Davidson thinks attribution of mental states without recourse to holistic and normative principles is conceptually inappropriate. Hence, the anomaly of the mental.

With this background in mind, let us return to "Mental Events." The 'apparent contradiction' that Davidson seeks to resolve stems from three principles, all of which Davidson accepts:

P1.   Principle of causal interaction: at least some mental events interact causally with physical events.

P2.   Principle of the nomological character of causality: Where there is causality, there must be a law; events related as cause and effect fall under strict laws.

P3.   Principle of the anomalism of the mental: there are no strict laws on the basis of which mental events can be predicted and explained.[5]

The first two principles seem to imply that at least some mental events can be predicted and explained on the basis of strict laws, while the third principle denies this. Davidson seeks to resolve the apparent contradiction by endorsing a token identity theory: Mental events (events taken to be particulars, tokens) are identical with physical events. At the same time, Davidson denies that there exists any type identity theory connecting mental properties with physical properties. The absence of type identity guarantees anomaly, whereas the truth of token identity guarantees that causal interaction between mental events and physical events can occur. This position—token identity without type identity—is what Davidson calls 'anomalous monism.'

Davidson's position was important when it first appeared (in the early 1970s) because, up until that time, no one had explicitly drawn the distinction between type identity and token identity. No one had shown how to be a materialist without being some kind of reductionist. Davidson's construal of events as particulars (tokens) enabled him to say that all events, including mental events, are physical events (have physical descriptions) without his having to say that there were any lawlike connections between types of physical event and types of mental event.

As it stands, anomalous monism is compatible with two states or events being alike physically yet different mentally. In order to avoid this counterintuitive consequence, Davidson introduced the notion of supervenience into the literature on the mind-body problem. Davidson endorses the idea that mental events supervene on physical events in the following sense: " ... mental characteristics are in some sense dependent, or supervenient, on physical characteristics. Such supervenience might be taken to mean that there cannot be two events alike in all physical respects but differing in some mental respect, or that an object cannot alter in some mental respect without altering in some physical respect."[6]

Anomalous monism, supplemented by supervenience, is supposed to reconcile the three apparently contradictory principles in the following way (here it is necessary to quote Davidson at some length):

> Causality and identity are relations between individual events no matter how described. But laws are linguistic; and so events can instantiate laws, and hence be explained or predicted in the light of laws, only as those events are described in one or another way. The principle of causal interaction deals with events in extension and is therefore blind to the mental-physical dichotomy. The principle of the anomalism of the mental concerns events described as mental, for events are mental only as described. The principle of the nomological character of causality must be read carefully: it says that when events are related as cause and effect, they *have descriptions* that instantiate a law. It does not say that every true singular statement of causality instantiates a law.[7]

So, we get the following picture: Mental events are physical events. These events may be causally related to other physical events, but such causal relations exist only insofar as the relevant events are subsumed under strict laws, and all strict laws connect types of event under physical descriptions. The fact that mental events have physical descriptions under which they are subsumed by laws means they can enter into causal transactions. The absence of laws connecting events under their mental descriptions, however, guarantees the anomaly of the mental. (See Figure 6.1 for a schematic view of Davidson's theory of how mental events can enter into causal relations with physical events such as body motions.)

Some further clarificatory remarks about Figure 6.1 will perhaps be helpful. Remember, the event described by M_1 *is* the event described by P_1, and the event described by M_2 *is* the event described by P_2. It's just that strict laws hold of these events in virtue of their satisfying P_1 and P_2, *not* in virtue of their satisfying M_1 and M_2. P_1 and P_2 are descriptions; P_1 doesn't cause P_2. But there is a strict law linking the event described by P_1 and the event described by P_2; moreover, this law links them in virtue of their satisfying *these* descriptions (and *not* in virtue of their satisfying M_1 and M_2).

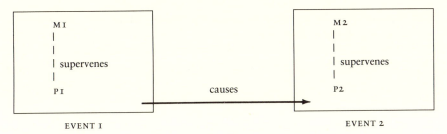

NOTE:

P1 = Physical description of EVENT 1 ('Neural state n')
P2 = Physical description of EVENT 2 ('Arm goes up')
M1 = Mental description of EVENT 1 ('Desire to wave')
M2 = Mental description of EVENT 2 ('Waving')

Some strict law connects Event 1 with Event 2 *under their physical descriptions*, P1 and P2. So Event 1 and Event 2 can be related as cause and effect. *No* strict law connects Event 1 and Event 2 under their mental descriptions, M1 and M2. The latter guarantees the anomalousness of the mental.

FIGURE 6.1   Davidson's theory of how mental events can enter into causal relations.

A complication enters the discussion at this point. The principle of the anomalism of the mental is said by Davidson to mean that there can be no strict psychophysical laws (laws connecting events under mental descriptions with events under physical descriptions) as well as that there can be no strict psychological laws (laws connecting events under different mental descriptions).[8] The denial that there can be strict psychophysical laws might be taken to mean either of two things:

1. There can be no strict lawlike connections between mental event types and physical event types, such as we get in the bridge principles of intertheoretic reduction.
2. There can be no strict laws connecting particular mental events and particular body motions under the mental descriptions of those events. (Actions are body motions, caused in a certain way, and have both physical and mental descriptions.)

Davidson apparently means to deny the existence of *both* kinds of psychophysical law.[9] The denial that there can exist the first kind of psychophysical law (bridge laws linking mental event types with physical event types) creates problems for Davidson when we consider the implications of Davidson's supervenience thesis.

Recall Davidson's first formulation of the supervenience thesis: "there cannot be two events alike in all physical respects, but differing in some mental respect."[10] This implies that the presence of the subvening physical property determines the presence of the supervening mental property. If this property-determination relation holds, then it would seem that there are laws of the bridge-principle type connecting every given mental property with every physical event type on which the mental event type supervenes. Supervenience, then, appears to conflict with the anomalism of the mental.[11]

There is this further problem with the picture painted by Davidson. Davidson's account of the causation of action may seem to accord too little causal relevance to the mental features of events. It may be said that the supervenient mental descriptions of events, on Davidson's account, seem not to be doing any causal-explanatory work; all the causal-explanatory work is being done by the subvenient physical descriptions that enter into strict causal laws. Doesn't this seem to make mental descriptions causally irrelevant, and isn't that counterintuitive? Don't we intuitively want to say that mental events play the causal roles they do *in virtue of their mental features,* that is, in virtue of satisfying their mental descriptions? (Look again at Figure 6.1; the mental descriptions of the events at issue appear to 'dangle', uninvolved in strict laws and accordingly uninvolved in causation.)

Davidson does want to maintain that reasons causally explain actions,[12] and this presumably requires that mental descriptions of events must do some real causal-explanatory work. If mental descriptions do any real causal-explanatory work, then it seems there must be genuinely lawlike statements of some kind, even if they do not amount to strict laws, connecting events under mental descriptions. This seems to be Davidson's approach. According to Davidson, there do exist rough generalizations containing psychological terms, and such generalizations may serve to back causal explanations of action. But such generalizations are not sufficiently strict (exceptionless) to be called genuine laws. The latter claim is intended by Davidson to preserve the anomalism of the mental in the face of his admission that explanation-backing psychophysical generalizations exist.

What shall we say by way of evaluating Davidson's views on these matters? My own conclusions are as follows: Davidson is surely on the right track with regard to mental causation. We definitely want to accord some genuine causal relevance to mental properties, and the way to do this seems to be to implicate mental properties in lawlike generalizations. (This will be discussed further in Chapter 8.) Davidson's supervenience claim also seems correct. (I argued earlier that supervenience is plausibly taken to be the relationship that obtains between brain states and mental states.) The problem with Davidson's picture is that supervenience conflicts with the anomalism of the mental. Either supervenience or anomalism must go, and in my opinion it is anomalism that must be rejected.

Recall that Davidson's main motivation for endorsing the anomalism of the mental appears to be his conviction that mental state attribution is essentially governed by holistic, normative constraints. Davidson can be seen as making the following argument: If there were strict psychophysical laws of the bridge-principle sort, then mental states could be assigned to a person one by one on the basis of that person's brain states; that is, holistic and normative constraints would not be necessary. But holistic and normative constraints are essential; they cannot be given up without giving up the mental as a conceptual realm. Therefore, there are no strict psychophysical laws of the bridge-principle sort.

While it seems clear to me that we cannot have supervenience (determination) without strict psychophysical laws of the bridge-principle sort, I am sympathetic to Davidson's claim that holistic constraints are essential features of the practice of assigning mental states to others. Can we have both holism and supervenience without anomaly? It seems possible that we might retain holism as an indispensable feature of mental state attribution without endorsing mental anomaly. This might be done by theorizing that *the brain itself is a holistic system.* Suppose, for example, that I believe Albuquerque is hot in August only if I have endless other beliefs. In this case, you couldn't look at the brain *locally* and figure out what I believe. Somehow, you'd have to look at *the whole brain.* The physical properties of the whole brain would determine what mental states I had. The question that arises is whether this 'holistic supervenience' is consistent with physical-mental supervenience as normally hypothesized. I do not immediately see why it wouldn't be, but this is an issue that begs for further investigation.

Of course, even if holistic supervenience is a coherent notion, it is wildly improbable that we will ever be able to read off mental states from a knowledge of the global physical state of the brain. While such a feat might be possible *in principle* if mind-brain supervenience holds, the extreme complexity of the brain states underlying particular holistic mental states renders it almost inconceivable that this could ever be done. For all practical purposes, the only way to determine the content of a given holistic brain state is to ask the person whose brain is in that state, What subjective states are you experiencing? It will accordingly remain true that mental states are always attributed to others on the basis of asking ourselves what it would be reasonable for them to believe, given their utterances and their behavior. We will never go around attributing mental states to people on the basis of their brain states. Holism and normativity will remain essential aspects of mental state attribution in practice, though they will not be in principle essential if supervenience holds. The anomalism of the mental, while it is, strictly speaking, false if supervenience holds, may thus reflect an insight of continuing validity.

DENNETT: THE INTENTIONAL STANCE

Dennett's theory of the nature of commonsense propositional attitude psychology appears, at first glance, to be a promising non-reductionist alternative to eliminative materialism, an account of the truth and legitimacy of commonsense psychology that does not demand that propositional attitude notions be reducible to anything statable in physical or functional terms.[13] As I did with Davidson's anomalous monism, I will describe Dennett's view in detail and make a few evaluative comments.

Dennett is popularly taken to be an instrumentalist with regard to propositional attitude states. He admits to a sort of instrumentalism but insists that his position is also a sort of realism:

> My *ism* is whatever *ism* serious realists adopt with regard to centers of gravity and the like, since I think beliefs (and some other mental items drawn from folk psychology) are *like that* in being *abstracta* rather than part of the 'furniture of the physical world' and in being attributed in statements that are *true* only if we exempt them from a certain familiar standard of literality.[14]

Dennett argues that attributions of beliefs and desires are 'true' in the same sense that it is 'true' that hand calculators perform arithmetical operations and in the same sense that it is 'true' that the gravitational attraction between the earth and the moon applies between the centers of gravity of those two bodies. He calls this type of truth 'veritas cum grano salis', or truth with a grain of salt.[15] Dennett holds that propositional attitudes are *not* determinately contentful internal physical states of the organism; rather, propositional attitudes are *abstracta,* attributed by predictors situated outside the organism for the purpose of predicting the behavior of the organism. Propositional attitude talk is legitimate because propositional attitude–based predictions are generally effective, but propositional attitude talk is only *true* in the *cum grano salis* sense.

Dennett explicitly and resolutely adopts a materialistic, scientific perspective toward both intentionality and consciousness. He clearly believes that some sort of objective theory of the nature of these mental phenomena is possible. Accepting the 'obvious truths' of common sense at face value, without seeking scientific verification or falsification, strikes Dennett as 'craven and dishonest',[16] a point upon which he agrees with such eliminativist theorists as Stich and Churchland. Dennett's opinion that belief and desire ought to be retained as meaningful categories does not stem from the fact that these notions are intimately involved in our 'manifest image' of the world. Rather, Dennett argues that empirical fact supports a scientifically respectable role for propositional attitude categories, despite the fact that these categories almost certainly will not reduce to any categories recognized by subpersonal cognitive psychology or by neurobiology.

The part of commonsense psychology that is worth saving from elimination, according to Dennett, is the practice of attributing propositional attitudes for predictive and explanatory purposes. He calls this practice 'intentional system theory'. Intentional system theory is a predictive calculus; it is 'abstract, idealizing, holistic, instrumentalistic'.[17] It is justified or legitimized by the simple fact that it works; predictions based upon propositional attitude attributions, more often than not, turn out to be correct.

In Dennett's terminology, a creature (whether organic or inorganic) whose behavior is accurately predictable by means of the attribution of propositional attitudes and the concomitant assumption of rationality is an 'intentional system'. To treat a system as rational and to attribute propositional attitudes to it in order to predict its behavior is to adopt 'the intentional stance' toward it. Intentional system theory is just the practice of using propositional attitude concepts and the concept of rationality in tandem to predict the behavior of intentional systems.

Intentional system theory does not attempt to reduce or analyze either propositional attitude notions or the notion of rationality. These notions are assumed by the user of intentional system theory to be pre-theoretically understood. Dennett describes intentional system theory as 'holistic logical behaviorism'.[18] According to Dennett, what we mean by attributing certain propositional attitudes to a system is that the system should rationally have certain behavioral dispositions, given its circumstances and its other beliefs and desires. A system really has the beliefs and desires occurring in the best (most predictively accurate) set of attributed beliefs and desires.[19] If there is no one most predictively accurate set of attributed propositional attitudes, then Dennett believes that there is no fact of the matter, between equally predictively accurate interpretations, as to what the system believes and desires.[20]

According to Dennett, the scientific value of intentional system theory consists in the following fact: Holistic propositional attitude attribution enables us to classify systems according to the rational behavioral dispositions they are apt to have in common. This succeeds in capturing certain regularities in the behavior of intentional systems that are objectively real. These regularities could not be captured without the use of intentional vocabulary:

> What spread around the world on July 20, 1969? The belief that a man had stepped on the moon. In no two people was the effect of the receipt of that information the same, and the causal paths eventuating in the state they all had in common were no doubt almost equally various, but the claim that therefore they all had nothing in common—nothing importantly in common—is false, and obviously so. There are indefinitely many ways one could reliably distinguish those with the belief from those without it. ... That is not something science should or could turn its back on.[21]

Oddly, Dennett does not believe that the predictive value of propositional attitude attribution stems from the fact that propositional attitudes are real states that cause behavior. Dennett thinks it is highly probable that whatever states turn out to be actually causally responsible for behavior will not be identifiable with propositional attitudes. He theorizes that the underlying physical organization of the system 'realizes' the intentional system, but the subpersonal states of the system are not individuated in the same manner as are propositional attitudes, and if these subpersonal states can be seen as having representational content at all, their content is derived from the content that is attributed at the level of the whole organism from the intentional stance.

Dennett denies that commonsense propositional attitude psychology is 'a theory in the classical mold'.[22] In saying this, he is claiming that commonsense psychology is not an empirical theory intended to explain behavior by positing causally relevant states of organisms. Commonsense psychology, for Dennett, is a stance, a strategy, an instrumentalistic method for the prediction of behavior, that is justified solely because it works.

While I agree with Dennett that commonsense propositional attitude psychology is not a theory in the classical sense, his approach has one major problem. This approach provides no explanation of why intentional-stance predictions of behavior are so often accurate. The most plausible explanation for the accuracy of intentional-stance predictions is that there really are physical states of the intentional system, identifiable with propositional attitudes, and that these states play causal roles in the genesis of behavior. But Dennett, with his characterization of propositional attitude states as *abstracta,* cannot easily avail himself of this explanation. The answer to the crucial question 'But why do intentional-stance predictions work?' remains, given Dennett's theory, a mystery.

I am also dissatisfied with Dennett's claim that there is no fact of the matter among equally predictively accurate attributed sets of propositional attitudes as to what propositional attitudes a system really has. This seems to me to ignore the 'system's' introspective access to its own beliefs and desires. To use an example due to Quine,[23] I might succeed in predicting the behavior of a person equally well on the hypothesis that he took himself to be hunting rabbits and on the hypothesis that he took himself to be hunting stages in the life cycles of rabbits. Surely, however, there is a fact of the matter, accessible to the hunter from his subjective point of view, as to whether he takes himself to be hunting rabbits or rabbit stages.

TOWARD A SATISFACTORY VERSION OF
NON-REDUCTIVE MATERIALISM

A satisfactory version of non-reductive materialism would avoid the pitfalls associated with Davidson's and Dennett's theories. It would clearly endorse the supervenience of mental states on brain states, and accordingly it would avoid endorsing Davidson's (evidently false) principle of mental anomalousness. It would also be realistic enough regarding propositional attitudes to give an account of mental causation.

There may be a common element in what seems to go wrong with Davidson's and Dennett's theories. Dennett and Davidson (in some of his moods) both see mental states as constructs attributed to persons by outside interpreters—they take a third-person approach to mental states.[24] As we saw earlier in connection with the critique of reductive mind-body theories, third-person approaches to the mental fall afoul of an arguably fatal difficulty. Such approaches ignore what is conceptually essential to the mental— its subjectivity, its accessiblity from the first-person point of view. In addition to endorsing realism about mental states and endorsing the supervenience of mental states on brain states, then, an essential feature of a satisfactory version of non-reductive materialism is that it must take mental properties to be essentially subjective.

＊ 7 ＊

In Defense of
Content Internalism

I HAVE SUGGESTED that a satisfactory version of non-reductive materialism (property dualism) would take mental properties to be essentially subjective and would include the thesis that mental properties supervene on physical states of brains. Let us call the claim that mental properties are essentially subjective thesis 1; let us call the idea that mental content supervenes locally on the brain thesis 2. I will now deflect objections to these two theses. (Let us call the combination of both theses 'internalism'. The denial of these two theses may be called 'externalism'.)

IS CONTENT REALLY SOMETHING SUBJECTIVELY KNOWN?

The standard objection to thesis 1 is that propositional attitudes can be dispositional or unconscious. (This objection to taking mental states to be essentially subjective was discussed briefly in Chapter 5 in connection with the introspective argument against eliminative materialism; what I say here will reinforce what I said there.) I acknowledge that we certainly use language this way; we say that a person has a particular belief when that belief is not presently before his or her conscious mind, and we use the Freudian language of unconscious belief and desire. But these ways of talking do not necessitate the rejection of my view that content is fundamentally first-person, subjective content.

In the case of a belief that is something a person would acknowledge believing if asked but which is simply not presently before the person's mind, I can say the following: Such a belief can be called to consciousness by appropriate stimuli. When conscious, the belief's content is something of which the believer is subjectively aware. Such beliefs can be accommodated within my view by making clear that the propositional attitudes it is correct to ascribe to a person depend upon the person's actual *and dispositional* states of

81

subjective awareness, dispositional states of subjective awareness being those that can be called to consciousness by asking the person, for example, 'What do you think about X?' when the person is not currently thinking about X. For example, it might be correct to say that I believe triangles have three sides, even at a time when I am not thinking about triangles. The three-sidedness of triangles is a matter I have thought about in the past, and the fact that triangles have three sides is stored in my memory. A belief such as my belief that triangles have three sides might be called a 'dispositional belief', since it is a belief I am disposed to acknowledge having when the topic of triangles comes up.

Dispositional beliefs should be distinguished from dispositions to believe.[1] I may be disposed to believe that the table in front of me is unlikely to burst into flames, but since the possibility of the table's bursting into flames has never crossed my mind, it seems wrong to say that I have a belief, even a dispositional belief, about the matter. If someone asks me, 'Do you now believe that the table is unlikely to burst into flames?' I may say, 'Yes,' but prior to the question's being posed, I had no belief; I had merely a disposition to believe.

Unconscious beliefs and desires in the Freudian sense present a slightly different problem. When we speak of a person as having certain unconscious beliefs and desires in this sense, we are not speaking literally. We are not saying that the person actually has internal states with such-and-such contents. Rather, we are saying, 'This person is behaving *as if* she had certain beliefs and desires'. Freud and his followers did not take themselves to be speaking metaphorically when attributing unconscious desires and beliefs to explain people's *prima facie* irrational behavior, but I am claiming that this is all anyone should take such talk to mean.

Suppose a woman repeatedly enters into destructive relationships with unhappily married men. Her own parents were unhappily married, and the men this woman chooses all bear an uncanny resemblance to her distant, unhappy father. A therapist might explain the woman's behavior utilizing the vocabulary of unconscious propositional attitudes: 'The woman unconsciously believes that her happiness depends upon rescuing her distant, unhappy father from his bad marriage'.

This might be an acute clinical diagnosis, but I submit that the language of unconscious beliefs and desires is metaphorical. The woman is behaving *as if* she had the relevant beliefs and desires, but it is not literally true that she has propositional attitudes with these contents. Talk of unconscious beliefs and desires in the Freudian sense, I submit, is derived from, and parasitic on, the basic use of propositional attitude concepts to pick out states of actual and potential subjective awareness.

DOES CONTENT SUPERVENE ON THE BRAIN?

Thesis 2, the idea that a person's mental states are determined by (supervenient on) his or her brain states at any given moment, is reinforced by the famous brain-in-the-vat thought experiment.

Suppose a physical duplicate of me could be created, exactly like me-at-the-present-moment right down to the molecules. Would such a duplicate have the same total state of mind I now have? Would the duplicate have all the same mental states?

Imagine, if you like, that a molecular duplicate of my brain exists somewhere, suspended in a vat of nutrient solution. That brain is embedded in a physical environment very different from mine; that brain also has a causal history very different from mine. But these factors would appear to be irrelevant to whether that brain has the same conscious states of awareness, apparent memories, and so on that I do. Whatever is going on in my conscious mind presumably is traceable to physical goings-on in my brain, and the vat-brain (by hypothesis) has exactly the same things going on inside.

Not everyone accepts the notion that a brain in a vat duplicating my brain states would thereby duplicate my mental states. Hilary Putnam has famously argued that a brain in a vat would not have thoughts about anything other than its deceptive input mechanisms. Having thoughts about subject matter s, for Putnam, presupposes having been in some sort of causal contact with subject matter s. Since the brain in the vat is causally isolated from a normal environment, its thoughts are not really about that environment; its thoughts are about whatever is actually causing its subjective states (electrodes hooked up to a computer, or whatever).[2]

Putnam's intuitions about brains in vats strike me as exceedingly odd. The brain in the vat has a subjective world; it imagines (perhaps) that it is in Albuquerque, New Mexico, eating excellent enchiladas with red chile. If the brain were to be hooked up to a vocalization device, it would say, "This red chile is great; New Mexico has the best red chile I've ever eaten." The natural thing to say is that the brain in the vat has thoughts about New Mexico and about red chile, even though the brain has always been in a vat in a laboratory and has never been close to New Mexico or to red chile. Similarly, when I dream of pink unicorns after eating too much red chile, it is natural to say that my dream was about pink unicorns, even though I have never been in contact with pink unicorns and even though pink unicorns are not what caused the dream. (Red chile caused the dream. But surely we don't want to say that the dream was about red chile!)

To those who reject Putnam's odd intuitions regarding aboutness, it seems plausible that mental states are about what they seem to be about; intentionality is essentially subjective.[3] And it seems clear that a person's subjective states must supervene locally on that person's brain states.

Consider: If a molecular duplicate of me-at-the-present-moment could be constructed, would it take itself to be me, in my present environment, doing what I am presently doing? To be specific, would it take itself to be typing words at a word processor, in a room just like the one I am in, and so on? Granted, it would be immensely difficult to duplicate my present brain states, but if this could be done, would the duplicate take itself to be in my exact situation? If your answer is 'yes', then you share the intuition that subjective mental content supervenes locally on the brain.

The thesis that propositional content does *not* supervene locally on the brain ('content is not in the head') has been defended, however, by Hilary Putnam, Tyler Burge, and Stephen Stich.[4] Let us look briefly at their respective arguments in order to understand why so many philosophers have been persuaded by this (to me, counterintuitive) doctrine.

Putnam asks us to imagine another planet, Twin Earth. Twin Earth is phenomenally identical to Earth; everything on Earth has a counterpart on Twin Earth that looks exactly the same. At this very moment, as I type at my word processor, my twin on Twin Earth is typing identical words at her identical word processor. Everything going on around me at any given moment is exactly duplicated by goings-on on Twin Earth. There is one difference, however, between Earth and Twin Earth: The clear liquid occurring in Twin Earth's rivers, lakes, and bathtubs is not H_2O, but another chemical compound, XYZ. Twin Earthers call this stuff 'water', and it looks, tastes, and behaves exactly like H_2O under normal conditions, but it isn't H_2O; it's XYZ.

Now, suppose I feel thirsty and think to myself, 'I would like a glass of water'. By hypothesis, my twin on Twin Earth, at the very same moment, thinks to herself, 'I would like a glass of water'. My twin and I are in identical states of subjective consciousness. Putnam asks us to suppose that my twin and I are in identical physical states.[5] Nevertheless, Putnam tells us, the commonsense intuition is that my twin and I are in *different mental states;* my desire is for water, and my twin's desire is for twin-water. Different substances in our physical environments, according to Putnam, make it the case that my twin and I have thoughts with *different contents,* even though my twin and I are physically identical and even though our subjective states are introspectively identical.

I cannot agree with Putnam that the commonsense intuition is that my twin and I are in mental states with different contents. On the contrary, the commonsense intuition seems to be that my twin and I are in content-identical mental states; we just happen to be embedded in different physical environments. Being embedded in a particular physical environment makes no difference in this case to the contents of my thoughts; such contents are determined by the states of my brain. Putnam, however, announces that his thought-experiment shows "Cut the pie any way you like, 'meanings' just ain't in the head!"[6]

Putnam's odd thesis about mental content can be traced to his (not-so-odd) doctrine regarding the meaning of natural kind terms such as 'water'. Putnam is in agreement with Kripke (see Chapter 2) as to how natural kind terms get their meaning. Natural kind terms are defined indexically; it is as if someone in the remote past of our planet pointed at a certain chemical compound and said, "*This stuff* shall be called 'water'." On Twin Earth, a different substance would have been pointed at; hence, the word 'water' has different meanings on Earth and on Twin Earth. In the case of a natural kind term such as 'water', the meaning of the term is the substance, species, etc., to which the term refers. I am willing to follow Putnam this far; what I fail to understand is why Putnam thinks that different *word-meanings* on the two planets are tantamount to different *thought-contents* on the part of twins.

Burge shows that the hypothesis of different physical environments, containing different natural kinds, is not crucial to running a Putnam-type thought-experiment. The same result can be reached by imagining two persons embedded in different linguistic communities. Burge asks us to imagine two persons (let us call them Oscar 1 and Oscar 2), each of whom has a belief he or she would express as "I have arthritis in my thigh." Oscar 1 belongs to our own linguistic community, in which 'arthritis' is correctly used to mean inflammation of the joints; inflammation of the thigh cannot be arthritis because the thigh is not a joint. Oscar 2, however, belongs to a deviant linguistic community in which 'arthritis' is used to refer to any inflammatory ailment, whether in joints or non-joints. In Oscar 2's community, one might truly assert, "I have arthritis in my thigh." Burge invites us to have the following intuition: Oscar 1 and Oscar 2 might be in mental states exactly the same from the subjective point of view; Oscar 1 and Oscar 2 might even be in physically identical brain states; still, Oscar 1 and Oscar 2 have different beliefs about their aching thighs. Since 'arthritis' means something different in their respective linguistic communities, the beliefs of Oscar 1 and Oscar 2 that they would express using the word 'arthritis' have different contents.

My reaction to Burge is the same as my reaction to Putnam. I must decline Burge's invitation to have the suggested intuition. It seems to me that the following is the right thing to say: Oscar 1 and Oscar 2 are in content-identical mental states; they just happen to be embedded in different communities that use the word 'arthritis' differently. Being embedded in a particular linguistic community makes no more difference to the contents of one's thoughts in this case than does being embedded in a particular physical environment in the Twin Earth case.

Stephen Stich makes the same kind of point as Burge. Stich suggests we imagine two men (call them Joe and George). Joe is American and George is

British. In America, the word 'chickory' is used to refer to a certain curly-leafed type of greens. In Britain, the word 'chickory' is used to refer to a certain smooth-leafed type of greens, the same stuff that Americans would call 'endive'. Imagine that the usage is simply switched, such that the curly-leafed stuff called 'chickory' by Americans is called 'endive' by the British and the smooth-leafed stuff called 'endive' by Americans is called 'chickory' by the British.

Suppose that Joe, the American, is invited to an American friend's home for dinner. Joe's friend offers him chickory salad. Joe has heard people say that chickory is bitter, though he doesn't know what chickory looks like and can't recall ever having tasted it. Joe declines the offer of chickory salad, tactlessly saying, 'Chickory is bitter'.

Likewise, George, the Englishman, is invited to a fellow Englishman's home for dinner. George is offered chickory salad. George has heard that chickory is bitter, but he doesn't know what chickory looks like and has never to his knowledge tried it. George declines the offer of chickory salad, saying, with a lack of tact equal to Joe's, 'Chickory is bitter'.

Stich asks his readers to consider this question: When Joe and George say 'Chickory is bitter', are they expressing the same belief or not? Stich reports that different people have different intuitions about this but that most seem to feel that Joe and George are expressing beliefs with different contents. Since Joe and George are equally mental blanks on the subject of chickory, it looks as if any difference in the content of their chickory beliefs must be accounted for by their embedding in different linguistic communities, not by any difference in their subjective states of consciousness as realized in their brains. To Stich, it appears that such examples show that Burge is probably correct: Mental content does not supervene on brain states.

It is a mistake to take Joe and George to be in different mental states. Suppose that Joe and George are true mental blanks on the subject of chickory. Neither Joe nor George associates any mental picture or descriptive data with the word "chickory." They have both just accepted the sentence 'Chickory is bitter' without any perceptual or descriptive knowledge of chickory. They don't even have a mental description of chickory as 'that stuff my linguistic community calls "chickory."' They have nothing in their heads but the word. In this case, Joe and George are in the same mental state with regard to chickory: the null mental state. The fact that they have memorized a certain sentence, 'Chickory is bitter', and are inclined to mouth that sentence does not indicate that the sentence expresses any belief at all.

But perhaps Joe and George do possess a mental description of chickory as 'that stuff my linguistic community calls "chickory."' In this latter case, Joe and George no longer have the null belief, but they do not have different thought-contents, either. It's just that their identical thought-contents are mentally indexed to different linguistic communities and hence to different substances.

What's going on here? Why do Burge, Putnam, and Stich have such peculiar intuitions? Burge, Putnam, and Stich take the content of what is said, on particular occasions when someone reports a belief, to give straightforwardly the content of what is believed by the speakers who say that. These theorists also believe that the truth-conditions for sentences attributing propositional attitudes tell us about the individuation conditions for thoughts, and those truth-conditions involve relations between an individual and his or her environment. In my view, these assumptions are false.

What a person says may or may not express accurately the way that person is conceiving of his or her situation. Further, thought contents are *not* properly individuated by reference to the truth-conditions of sentences used to attribute propositional attitudes to the thinker. Every subjective thought has its own unique truth-condition. (A thought's truth-condition is just what would have to be the case for that thought to be true.) The sentences used to attribute propositional attitudes to a person may or may not capture accurately the truth-conditions of the person's thoughts.

The content of someone's thoughts is *what that person is experiencing subjectively;* it is not the set of that-clauses we would use in language to express what the person is experiencing subjectively. Using 'content' to mean both *what is attributed* and *the linguistic items used to attribute it* has led to much bad philosophy. Once we bring in that-clauses (natural language's device for characterizing thought-content), we bring in words, and some words, in some contexts, may get their reference from factors other than the subjective intentions of the speaker. A speaker's words may get their reference from the intentions of listeners, as is shown by the 'Ich bin ein Berliner' example (Kennedy succeeded in saying that he was a jelly roll, whereas he had no intention to say such a thing), or a speaker's words may get their reference from the intentions of his or her linguistic community in general, as is shown by examples of beliefs involving natural kinds such as water. But it remains true that the subjective content and phenomenal experience of both the speaker and the other relevant parties are in the head (where else could they sensibly be said to be?).

In giving an account of the nature of commonsense propositional attitude psychology, we must continually remind ourselves that what is ascribed when we attribute propositional attitudes to ourselves and others is content in the subjective, first-person sense. That-clauses and their truth-conditions are not the contents of thoughts. That-clauses are linguistic devices that may capture thought-content more or less accurately. The truth-condition of a particular that-clause may or may not match the truth-condition of the thought the that-clause is used to characterize.

Once the confusion between that-clauses and subjective mental content is cleared away, Putnam, Burge, and Stich may be seen to be mistaken in their claim that thought-content does not supervene locally on brain states. If what we mean by 'content' is subjective, first-person content, then content supervenes locally on the brain. To rephrase Putnam: If it ain't in the head, it ain't content!

The issues discussed in this chapter are difficult. In order to clarify the debate between internalists and externalists about mental content, I close this chapter with a brief pseudo-Socratic dialogue.

A DIALOGUE CONCERNING BELIEF AND CONTENT

Socrates and one of his less well-known followers, Simplicio, have rematerialized in the United States in the late twentieth century. They have learned English and familiarized themselves with modern culture, history, and science. Delighted to learn that Plato's reports of his views are still read and studied, Socrates has secured a professorship at a certain university in Northern California. Simplicio has enrolled as a graduate student. The following conversation takes place in Socrates' office.

SIMPLICIO: Socrates? May I come in and talk with you?

SOCRATES: By the dog, Simplicio, it's good to see you. I've been sitting here trying to write something, and you know how I dislike writing and prefer conversation. They tell me I must write and publish articles in order to keep this job. It looks like I'm going to be a failure as a philosopher in these times—ha! So, what's on your mind?

SIMPLICIO: I'm puzzled by the views of my teachers. I'm especially puzzled by what they say about belief.

SOCRATES: What do they say about belief that puzzles you?

SIMPLICIO: Well, you are familiar with the materialist orientation of these philosophers. They say that beliefs are physical states of brains. That, I can accept. But they also say that the content of beliefs does not supervene on physical states of brains. Content is not in the head, they say. It is this I don't understand. How can beliefs be in the head, and their content somewhere else?

SOCRATES: We must take care, Simplicio, to define our terms. What is a belief? What is the content of a belief? What would it be for the contents of beliefs to supervene on physical states of brains? These matters must be clarified before I can address your question.

SIMPLICIO: As I understand it, beliefs are states that enter into the explanation of action in a certain way, usually in combination with desires. The mode of explanation is usually taken to be causal.[7] For example, I came to your office today because I believed you were in your office, and I desired to ask you a question. My belief and my desire jointly caused me to come here.

SOCRATES: Do beliefs necessarily enter into the explanation of action? Might I have a belief that never entered into the explanation of any action of mine? For example, suppose I believe that Neptune is a cold planet. I read this in a book, perhaps. But I never talk to anyone about Neptune or do anything that proceeds from this belief. Still, I have the belief, do I not?

SIMPLICIO: It seems so, Socrates. I should have said that beliefs may, but need not, enter into the explanation of actions.

SOCRATES: Are beliefs states of consciousness, then?

SIMPLICIO: Not necessarily. Some are dispositional. For example, you now have a dispositional belief that triangles are three-sided figures, but this belief was not before your conscious mind until I mentioned it. Perhaps we should say that beliefs are states of conscious awareness, or non-occurrent states that may be brought to conscious awareness given appropriate stimuli.

SOCRATES: Perhaps, too, we must distinguish dispositional beliefs from dispositions to believe. I recall a certain sage from Nebraska giving an excellent talk on this topic.[8] Consider, Simplicio: Do you now believe that I am not wearing a toga? I am not in fact wearing a toga, having given up the Greek mode of dressing for the American mode. Chances are, however, that whether I was or was not wearing a toga never crossed your mind until I just mentioned it. This is different from the dispositional belief about triangles having three sides; I had, at many points in the past, explicitly entertained that belief, so it was truly a belief of mine even when not before my conscious mind. But you have the disposition to believe many things that have never before crossed your mind, such as that I am not now wearing a toga, Buckingham Palace is not filled with pickles,[9] and so on.

SIMPLICIO: I agree, Socrates; these mere dispositions to believe must not be counted among a person's beliefs.

SOCRATES: Very well. Now, what is the content of a belief?

SIMPLICIO: I'm not sure. I think I can say the following with confidence, however: Whatever content is, it has something to do with the intentionality of beliefs. 'Intentionality' means aboutness. Beliefs are about something; to be about something is to have content.

SOCRATES: So, suppose I believe there is a tree outside my office window, which there is. This belief is about a particular tree. But what, exactly, is the belief's content? Is the content the tree itself, the thing the belief is about?

SIMPLICIO: Not exactly, Socrates. According to some, the content of your belief is a proposition, an abstract entity of some kind, named by the words 'that there is a tree outside Socrates' office window at time t'. Some say the proposition contains the tree itself; others say it contains no concrete objects.

SOCRATES: If I understand you, these philosophers suggest that believing is a relation between a person and a proposition, a proposition being either a wholly abstract object or a combination abstract-and-concrete object?

SIMPLICIO: That's the general idea, yes.

SOCRATES: I'm not sure I see how this illuminates the question of what belief content is. I am told that a belief's content is some sort of abstraction, or an abstraction with concrete things somehow stuck into it. This is supposed to help?

SIMPLICIO: Well, there is a sage in New Jersey[10] who gives a different account. According to this wise man, believing is not a relation to a proposition; it is a relation to a mental representation. A mental representation is something wholly concrete; it is a physical state of the brain. It obtains its content via causal relations with the world outside the believer's brain. The content of this mental representation, then, is just its meaning, or that which it represents.

SOCRATES: Ah. But now, Simplicio, it seems that we are back in the same soup as before. This mental representation is just the belief itself, and how does it get its content? By means of a relation to something, its meaning. Presumably this meaning is either an abstract entity, or a combination of abstract entities and real objects. So, we're back with these mysterious propositions.

SIMPLICIO: But why must abstract entities be involved? Couldn't the content of a belief be wholly accounted for on the basis of causal relations with concrete things?

SOCRATES: Fairly obviously, no. For I may have beliefs that are not about any concrete things at all. For example, I may have beliefs about triangles and their properties. Even beliefs involving real, concrete individuals will involve properties and relations, which are abstract. There is the further problem that some beliefs are about imaginary concrete entities, such as Pegasus and Zeus.

SIMPLICIO: Hmm. I shall have to think about that.

SOCRATES: Let us leave aside the question of the nature of content; perhaps something will emerge later in the discussion to illuminate it. Why don't we move on to our next preliminary question: What would it be for the contents of beliefs to supervene on brain states?

SIMPLICIO: On this matter I am well prepared. There are three main varieties of supervenience: strong, weak, and global.[11] While a variety of views have been proposed, it is generally agreed that mind-brain supervenience, if it obtains, is most plausibly taken to be strong supervenience. This means that every time a mental property is exemplified, it is realized in some physical property or other, and whenever one of the physical properties in the supervenience base occurs, the supervening mental property is necessarily present.

SOCRATES: Let me make sure I understand this. Mental properties include content properties, such as believing that there is a tree outside the window. If this strong supervenience relation holds, then my property of believing that there is a tree outside the window is realized in some physical state of my brain. Anytime that physical state type is tokened, whether in my brain or in someone else's brain, the subject of that state necessarily believes that there is a tree outside the window. Likewise, Simplicio, your property of believing that there is a tree outside the window is realized in some physical state of your brain, in all likelihood a different physical state type than that which realizes the same belief in me. If that physical state type, the one tokened in your head, is ever tokened in someone else's head, then the subject of that state necessarily believes that there is a tree outside the window.

SIMPLICIO: Correct, Socrates. An admirable account of strong supervenience.

SOCRATES: I notice that the supposition of strong supervenience seems to underlie the famous brain-in-the-vat thought-experiment. According to that thought-experiment, if a molecular duplicate of my brain could be made and kept alive in a vat of nutrient solution, and its states from moment to moment could be made to match mine molecule for molecule, that brain would have my exact sequence of mental states; from its subjective point of view, it would take itself to be me, living my life. Is that not so?

SIMPLICIO: Correct, Socrates. But the brain-in-the-vat thought-experiment is usually used to make a point about epistemic skepticism—how do we know the real world exists, how do we know we are not brains in vats—whereas currently we are not entertaining any skeptical hypothesis; we're just trying to figure out what the relationship might be between brain states and belief contents.

SOCRATES: Quite so. Now, let us continue. You tell me that your teachers insist that this supervenience relationship does not hold between physical properties of brains and content properties. Have you any idea what their arguments might be?

SIMPLICIO: One philosopher argues as follows: Imagine another planet, Twin Earth. Twin Earth is, in all phenomenal respects, exactly like Earth. At this very moment on Twin Earth, for example, there is a Twin Simplicio talking to a Twin Socrates, uttering the very same noises I now utter. Twin Simplicio's brain states are molecule-for-molecule identical to mine; Twin Socrates' brain states are molecule-for-molecule identical to yours. Our twins are sitting in a twin of this office, in a twin of this building, in a twin of this university, and so on. Everything is exactly the same, such that, if you were instantaneously transported to Twin Earth and substituted in the place of your twin, you'd never notice the slightest difference; you'd think you never left Earth.

SOCRATES: Is this Twin Earth another so-called possible world?

SIMPLICIO: No; it is supposed to be an imagined physical location rather than a possible way things might have been.

SOCRATES: Good; talk about 'possible worlds' confuses me. Continue.

SIMPLICIO: As I said, Twin Earth is phenomenally identical to Earth, but there is a difference at the subvisual level. The clear liquid that Twin Earthers drink, swim in, wash with, and so on, the stuff they call 'water', is not the chemical compound H_2O; it is another compound, XYZ.

SOCRATES: I detect an inconsistency in the example. People's brain cells are mostly water. If the stuff called 'water' in these two planets is chemically different, my twin and I cannot possibly be in molecule-for-molecule identical brain states.

SIMPLICIO: That doesn't matter; the same sort of thought-experiment could be run using some substance that doesn't occur in the human body.

SOCRATES: Continue, then.

SIMPLICIO: Suppose, Socrates, that neither you nor your twin knows anything about the chemical composition of the stuffs called 'water' in your respective worlds. You think to yourself the thought that water is wet. Simultaneously, on Twin Earth, Twin Socrates thinks to himself the thought he would phrase as "water is wet." According to the philosopher who made up this example,[12] Socrates and Twin Socrates have thoughts with different contents, because the stuff called 'water' on Earth and the stuff called 'water' on Twin Earth are different substances. Socrates and Twin Socrates are in identical brain states, supposedly, yet their beliefs have different contents. So, belief content doesn't supervene on brain states.

SOCRATES: This is truly absurd! Who would think that Twin Socrates and I had beliefs with different contents, merely because we happened to be in chemically different environments? Twin Socrates and I are in identical subjective states; our brains are supposedly in identical physical states ... my intuition is that Twin Socrates and I have the same belief content. The philosopher who made up this example has peculiar intuitions.

SIMPLICIO: I tend to agree with you, Socrates. Nonetheless, most of the
philosophical community seems to have the same peculiar intuitions
as the author of the Twin Earth example. Another philosopher
presents a similar thought experiment to show, supposedly, that
different linguistic communities can have the same content-altering
effect as different physical environments.

SOCRATES: Tell me about it. This should be entertaining, if not
instructive.

SIMPLICIO: This philosopher asks us to imagine two men. On the one
hand, there is a man who has a belief he would express as "I have
arthritis in my thigh." He happens to live in a linguistic community in
which the word 'arthritis' is properly used only to mean
inflammation of a joint. The thigh is not a joint, so this man can't
really have arthritis in his thigh. On the other hand, we have another
man who also has a belief he would express as "I have arthritis in my
thigh," but this second man happens to live in a linguistic community
where the word 'arthritis' is properly used to refer to any
inflammatory ailment, whether in joints or in other body parts. So,
this second man can truly assert, "I have arthritis in my thigh."
According to the author of this example,[13] the two men have beliefs
with different contents, even if, by hypothesis, their respective beliefs
expressed by the words 'I have arthritis in my thigh' are realized in
physically identical states of their brains. Again, we are supposed to
conclude that the contents of beliefs don't supervene on physical
states of brains.

SOCRATES: I see what's going on. These examples are superficially
clever, but their authors are trading on an ambiguity in the term
'content'. Notice, 'content' might mean the believer's state of
subjective awareness when he entertains the belief at issue. In this
first sense of content, like contents evidently do supervene on like
brain states. This is, I think, the simpler and more intuitive sense of
'content', but perhaps people's intuitions differ. 'Content' might also
be used for the standard meaning of the sentence, or that-clause, used
to characterize in language the subjective states of a believer. In this
second sense of 'content', content does not supervene on brain states,
because the words in the sentence or that-clause used to characterize
the content of a particular belief may get their standard meaning
from factors other than the subjective intentions of the particular
believer. In the Twin Earth example, the word 'water' gets its
meaning from the intentions of a particular community to refer to a
particular local substance. In the arthritis example, the word
'arthritis' gets its meaning from the intentions of a particular
community to refer to one sort of ailment or other.

SIMPLICIO: By Zeus, Socrates, I believe you're onto something.

SOCRATES: Equivocation, indeed, is a subtle fallacy. Content in the first sense, a believer's subjective state, is claimed to supervene on brain states. It is then shown that content in the second sense, the standard meanings of the words used to characterize a given believer's subjective content in language, does not supervene on brain states. The philosophical community concludes that a great point has been established: Content does not supervene on brain states! But in fact, nothing has been proved, because the crucial word 'content' has been employed in two senses in the same argument.

SIMPLICIO: May I suggest some useful terminology? Let us use the term 'subjective content' for content in the first sense, the believer's subjective state; let us use the term 'wide content' for content in the second sense, the standard meanings of the that-clauses used to characterize the believer's mental state. By using different terms for the two different senses of 'content', we can avoid equivocation.

SOCRATES: Fine. Now, notice: Wide content is intended to capture subjective content in words. Subjective content is prior to the ascription of wide content, and the wide content ascribed may be more or less accurate in capturing the subjective content of the thought. It appears obvious that when I characterize my own beliefs, or someone else's beliefs, in language, the words I use may have varying degrees of success is communicating the essence of the thought. Beliefs surely have truth conditions even before those beliefs are put into words; a belief's truth condition is whatever would have to be the case for that belief to be true. The ascription of wide content attempts to communicate the truth condition of a belief but may not do so accurately.

SIMPLICIO: What you say seems correct to me, Socrates.

SOCRATES: We have made some progress; we have determined that there is a sense in which content does supervene on brain states, and we have agreed that this narrow or subjective content is the primary thing to which truth conditions attach. The latter point is of great importance. No sentence can have a truth condition unless humans agree by convention that the words involved in that sentence shall be used to mean particular things. To use a word to mean a particular thing is to have a certain intention. To have a certain intention is to entertain a certain subjective content. Sentences, thus, have truth conditions only derivatively; the contentfulness of symbols is based upon the subjective contentfulness of thoughts.

SIMPLICIO: Professor Searle has stressed this; he calls the subjective contentfulness of thoughts, from which all other contentfulness is derived, 'intrinsic Intentionality'.[14]

SOCRATES: Searle is correct about this. There is no other intelligible account, it seems to me, of how words and other symbols acquire their meanings. But let us review the results of our discussion so far. It follows from what has been said that the intrinsic intentionality of thoughts, from which the intentionality or truth-evaluability of sentences derives, is the same thing as the subjective content of thoughts, and such subjective content, in all probability, supervenes on brain states. Is this not correct?

SIMPLICIO: Correct, Socrates. I am still confused, however, as to why certain of my teachers say the implausible things they say about belief and content. Professor Davidson presented us with a thought-experiment recently that baffled me. Davidson asked us to imagine the following: Davidson is standing in a swamp. Lightning strikes a dead tree nearby. Davidson's body is disintegrated into its elements. Entirely by coincidence, and out of different molecules, a duplicate of Davidson is formed where the tree once stood. This duplicate of Davidson goes to Davidson's house, takes over Davidson's job, and assumes Davidson's life; it talks and acts just like Davidson, and nobody knows it is really the Swampman and not Davidson.[15]

SOCRATES: Weird. How do these philosophers think of such things?

SIMPLICIO: Now, Davidson has the intuition that the Swampman doesn't mean anything when it uses the word 'house'—or, indeed, when it uses any word. The Swampman, according to Davidson, doesn't mean anything by the sounds it makes; further, the Swampman doesn't have any thoughts at all.[16]

SOCRATES: Hmm. Davidson seems to be assuming that thought-content is essentially something in words, an assumption we objected to just now. But, leaving that point aside for the moment, tell me: Does Davidson give any argument for the claim that the Swampman doesn't mean anything by its words?

SIMPLICIO: Just one. He says that words and sentences derive their meaning from the context in which they are learned by language users. 'House', when uttered by a given individual, means a particular sort of structure because this word was uttered in the presence of that particular sort of structure during the individual's word-learning period. The Swampman never had a word-learning period; it makes the sound 'house' in the presence of houses only because it seems to remember that 'house' is the word for that sort of structure. But the Swampman's memories, including its memories of word-meanings, are all fake; the Swampman doesn't remember anything from the period before Davidson was zapped, because the Swampman didn't even *exist* before Davidson was zapped. Davidson apparently thinks that an unbroken historical chain must exist linking a person to the occasion on which that person's words were learned in an appropriate context; otherwise, the person can't mean anything by his words. In the case of the Swampman, the historical chain stretching back to Davidson's learning of words has been broken.

SOCRATES: But why should the breaking of the historical chain make such a drastic difference as to what the Swampman can mean by its words? My own intuitions are at odds with Davidson's. When the Swampman says, "Come to my house for dinner on Saturday evening," it seems to me that it means something quite definite by its utterance.

SIMPLICIO: I agree with you, Socrates.

SOCRATES: Further, why does Davidson hold that the Swampman doesn't have any thoughts? By hypothesis, the Swampman is an exact duplicate of Davidson; presumably this means it started off its existence with brain states exactly like those Davidson had at the time of Davidson's unfortunate disintegration. The Swampman, from its subjective point of view, would seem to have all of Davidson's memories; it would seem to recognize all of Davidson's friends; it would hold all of Davidson's philosophical views. Why don't these states of mind constitute thoughts?

SIMPLICIO: I share your bafflement. Has it occurred to you, Socrates, that if Davidson is right about the Swampman, then you and I have no thoughts, and we mean nothing by our words, since we, like the Swampman, only recently materialized in this time and place?

SOCRATES: You're right; and this gives me even more confidence that Davidson's view is just wrong. When I first materialized in this time and place, I looked around in great surprise. I remember uttering, under my breath, the ancient Greek equivalent of "Where am I? This is not Athens." When a woman passing by offered me coins, I refused them, saying to her, "I am not a beggar; I am Socrates, the philosopher." She did not understand my Greek, and seemed to think I was a madman. But from my own point of view, it certainly seemed to me that I was having genuine thoughts and that I was using my words with their normal meanings. Can one be mistaken as to whether one is really having thoughts? I think not.

SIMPLICIO: You and I seem to agree, Socrates, that the way in which one acquires one's knowledge of word-meanings is not crucial to the issue of whether one can use words with meaning; nor is it crucial to the issue of whether one can have contentful thoughts. You and I, and the Swampman if it exists, acquired our knowledge of word-meanings in a most peculiar way—by being materialized with our brains in particular physical states. This is not the normal way to acquire word-meanings, but its abnormality does not vitiate the fact that our thoughts possess intrinsic intentionality. It is this intrinsic intentionality that enables us to use words with meaning, and so, our deviant causal background does not vitiate our ability to use words with meaning.

SOCRATES: I could not have said it better myself, Simplicio.

SIMPLICIO: I now recall a puzzling claim once made by the same sage who invented Twin Earth.[17] According to this sage, a brain in a vat could not have thoughts about anything external to itself and its deceptive input mechanisms. I now see that this sage must have an intuition similar to Davidson's; he must believe that one's words can have meaning only in virtue of a history during which one was embedded within a particular physical and social environment. You and I, Socrates, do not have this intuition, and we believe that the only argument in its favor is faulty.

SOCRATES: Agreed. And now, Simplicio, if you will excuse me, I must stop talking and return to my struggle to write something. Publish or perish, you know.

SIMPLICIO: Of course. I will go now and present myself to Davidson as a living counterexample to his view.

❧ 8 ❧

The Problem of
Mental Causation

MENTAL CAUSATION AND SUBSTANCE DUALISM

One of the most obvious problems faced by a substance dualist view of the mind is the following: How does the mind, which is supposed to be a non-physical, spiritual substance, interact causally with the physical body? Causal interactions between body and mind clearly do take place. When my body is injured, my mind perceives pain. When light enters my eyes, my mind perceives visual images. These are examples of the body causing things to happen in the mind. The causal process also runs from mind to body, as in cases of volition. For example, my mind decides that I will type the word 'cat' and my body obeys; my fingers move in the appropriate manner and I type the word 'cat'. If one believes (as Descartes believed) that the mind and the body are two distinct substances, the essence of body being its extended-ness in space and the essence of mind being its activity of rational thought, the problem arises: How do two such different substances interact causally?

Descartes himself did not really propose a solution to this problem. He merely suggested where the supposed mind-body interaction might take place: a small gland in the head called the pineal gland. Descartes observed that, in general, humans exhibit bilateral symmetry: There are two eyes, two ears, two arms, two legs, two brain hemispheres, and so on. Yet there is only one pineal gland. Descartes hypothesized that in this gland, the two physical images from the two retinas of the two eyes (for example) might somehow combine to produce the single image perceived by the mind.[1]

This is not very good reasoning. The pineal gland is not the only exception to the general bilateral symmetry of the human body. For example, there is only one mouth, only one navel, only one heart, etc. Yet Descartes did not suppose that the mind has some special connection with the mouth, the na-vel, the heart, or any of the other non-dual bodily features. What is so special about the pineal gland? Descartes offers no illumination.

Descartes does say that the soul is "united to all portions of the body con-

99

jointly" rather than having exclusive residence in the pineal gland. It is a mistake, according to Descartes, to suppose that the mind is anywhere at all, since the mind has no extension in space, yet somehow the mind is "joined to the whole body" and in the pineal gland the mind "exercises its functions more particularly" than in any other part of the body.[2] These assertions are puzzling and inconsistent. One is forced to conclude that Descartes's attempt to account for mind-body interaction does not represent his finest intellectual hour.

Another substance dualist, of approximately the same historical period as Descartes, who attempts to give an account of mental causation is Nicholas Malebranche. Malebranche was dissatisfied with Descartes's obscure notion that mind and body could interact causally in the pineal gland. According to Malebranche, there are no true causal relations in nature. The only true cause, according to Malebranche, is "the constant and immutable will of the Creator."[3] This doctrine applies to mental causation as follows: When I will to move my arm, and my arm subsequently moves, there is no genuine causal connection between my act of will and my arm's motion. Rather, my act of will is the *occasion* for God to cause my arm to move. Likewise, when Carlos bites me and I feel pain, there is no true causal connection between the bite and the pain. The bite is the occasion for God to insert a pain into my mind. This view is called *occasionalism*.

As we saw earlier (Chapter 1), there are plenty of reasons to reject substance dualism. The difficulty of explaining mind-body interaction on the hypothesis of substance dualism is just one problem among many. Given that the rational course is to reject substance dualism, even on grounds having nothing to do with causal interaction, we needn't be overly concerned with the problem of mental causation as it arises for a substance dualist.

Before we look at the problem of mental causation as it arises within the modern materialist metaphysics, let us examine one more historical approach to the problem of mental causation: that of Gottfried Leibniz.

LEIBNIZ ON MENTAL CAUSATION

The seventeenth-century philosopher and scientist Gottfried Leibniz was not a substance dualist. Leibniz's metaphysical system is unique: He holds that what appears to us to be a physical world is actually composed of tiny, self-contained atoms of mental substance; he calls these mental atoms *monads*.[4] Leibniz holds that each monad is actually an independent substance, since no monad depends upon any other monad for its existence or its attributes.

Each monad is a tiny mind, but most monads are not conscious of very much. Other monads have a greater level of awareness. Leibniz would say that an inanimate object such as a table is composed wholly of monads possessing a low level of consciousness. An animal or person, however, contains one dominant monad, its soul-monad, with a comparatively high level of consciousness. Each monad has desires and perceptions to some degree, but, according to Leibniz, "the monads have no windows through which something can enter or leave."[5]

Consider how voluntary action would have to work, given Leibniz's metaphysical system. My soul-monad desires a cup of coffee. Subsequently, all the other monads making up my body move in concert with my soul-monad into the kitchen, where I pour myself a cup of coffee. But how do the monads making up my body know what to do? After all, they "have no windows" by which my soul-monad's desire might be communicated to them; each of them is an independent substance, not in causal interaction with any other substance. This presented a puzzle for Leibniz, which he solved as follows: Since there is no causal interaction or other communication among monads, it must be the case that monads only act *as if* they are in causal communication with one another. The monads act in *pre-established harmony*. In the beginning, God set it up so that all the monads behave precisely as if there are causes and effects in the natural world. But there really are none. The only true cause is God, who, in the beginning, caused the best out of all possible worlds to be actualized.

Leibniz's doctrine of pre-established harmony is similar in some ways to Malebranche's occasionalism. Leibniz's view is more elegant, however, in that it does not require constant intervention by God in the natural world; God 'wound up' the world in the beginning, and events unfold as God chooses, without His constant interference.

SOMETHING TO BEAR IN MIND

The apparently bizarre nature of the above-mentioned historical approaches to the problem of mental causation is perhaps to be explained on the grounds that these theorists were grappling with a grave metaphysical problem: Given the assumption that mind and body are two essentially different substances, one substance extended in space and the other not, how could mind-body interaction possibly take place? Malebranche attempted to solve this problem by denying genuine causal interaction in the natural world while admitting the existence of both substances. Leibniz attempted to solve the problem in a more radical way by denying both the existence of genuine causal interaction and the existence of physical substance. Because our modern metaphysics is materialist, we do not see the necessity for theories such as pineal gland interactionism, occasionalism, and pre-established harmony. Hence, these approaches may strike us as bizarre or even amusing. We should not fall into the trap, however, of dismissing Descartes, Malebranche, and Leibniz as crackpots or minor thinkers. A useful slogan to remember is this: When you find a philosopher saying something that seems wild, look for the motivation!

The problem of mental causation emerges in a new form within a non-reductive materialist view of the mind such as that I have defended in earlier chapters. Let us now turn to consideration of that problem.

MENTAL CAUSATION AND PROPERTY DUALISM

Consider a position on the mind-body problem defended by nineteenth-century philosopher Thomas Huxley: *epiphenomenalism.* According to Huxley, mental properties of brain states (consciousness, qualia, propositional content) are *causally inert.* These mental properties may be caused by physical features of the brain, but they themselves do not cause anything.[6]

Huxley first applies this thesis to non-human animals. He finds it plausible to suppose that non-human animals are 'conscious automata'. That is, animals may well have mental states (feelings, beliefs, etc.) but they operate on a purely physiological, stimulus-response basis; their beliefs and feelings are causally inert accompaniments of the causally necessitated (determined) motions of their bodies.

Huxley believes humans are not qualitatively different from other animals. Humans, like other animals, are 'conscious automata'. Our mental properties are mere *epiphenomena,* caused by physical properties of our brains, but not themselves causally efficacious. Mental properties just 'hang around' (so to speak); they don't do any causal work.

Suppose Huxley is right; epiphenomenalism is true. Then, I am not at this moment typing because of my desire to finish my book; rather, I am at this moment typing because various physiological things are happening in my brain and nervous system. My desire to finish my book is just an epiphenomenal by-product of whatever is happening in my neurons; the intuition that the desire is playing a causal role is just an illusion. Likewise, it is not the case that Bill marries Hilary because he likes her forceful character, her intelligence, and her pretty hair; rather, Bill's marriage is the causally determined product of his genes and his chemistry. That he makes conscious choices in this area is illusory. Bill's mental states are causally inert; so are yours and mine. We are deluded in thinking we pilot ourselves through the world as agents; we are just robots who suffer from the delusion that our conscious states make a difference as to what we do.

One doesn't want to believe that epiphenomenalism is true. Yet, if one defends the thesis that mental properties supervene on physical properties of brains, one faces the challenge of explaining why one's position does not commit one to epiphenomenalism.

To see why property dualism may appear to lead to epiphenomenalism, consider the following: It is clear that in any given causal transaction, some properties are causally relevant and other properties are not. Suppose I suffer from depression, and my psychiatrist prescribes Prozac. The Prozac capsules are ovoid in shape. I take these ovoid capsules for a couple of weeks, and the depression lifts. Clearly, certain chemical properties of the Prozac capsules caused the lifting of my depression. The ovoid shape of the capsules, however, had nothing to do with the fact that my depression lifted.

Now, suppose I decide to get a cup of coffee, and I get up out of my chair, go into the kitchen, and pour myself some coffee. Possibly, it was the physical properties of my brain and body that caused me to go into the kitchen and get coffee; possibly, the mental property supervening on those physical properties (the subjectively experienced desire for coffee) was just as causally irrelevant as the ovoid shape of the Prozac pills.

Recall that, according to the supervenience doctrine I have defended, the mental property of desiring coffee is not identical with any physical property; the mental property is essentially that of being in a particular sort of subjective state. But subjectivity seems to have no causal powers *qua* subjectivity; whatever causal powers subjective states possess presumably are the causal powers of their physical realization bases. It looks as if, on any particular occasion when a person seems to do something because of a desire for coffee, all the real causal work is being done by the physical property that happens to be subvenient on that occasion; the supervening mental property is just 'hanging around', not playing any causal role of its own. The same may be said about any occasion when a person seems to perform an action for a reason. If reasons are just brain states, it would seem to be the physical properties of these brain states that do the causal work; the mental properties of these brain states are causally irrelevant, epiphenomenal. This, in a nutshell, is the modern problem of mental causation.

FODOR AND KIM ON MENTAL CAUSATION

What accounts for the fact that certain chemical properties of Prozac capsules are causally relevant to the depression-lifting effect of the capsules, whereas the ovoid shape of the capsules is causally inert? The answer to this question seems to concern the existence of lawlike generalizations. No lawlike generalization connects the swallowing of ovoid bodies with the lifting of depression, while there is a lawlike generalization connecting the swallowing of a certain chemical compound with the lifting of depression. If a certain number of depressed persons swallow the chemical compound that is the active ingredient in Prozac, a certain proportion of those persons will experience improvement in their depressed mental state. If a certain number of depressed persons swallow assorted ovoid bodies, no statistically significant effect upon their depression is to be expected. Because of such facts, we can *causally explain* a person's relief from depression on the grounds that the person took the active ingredient of Prozac; we cannot causally explain a person's relief from depression on the grounds that the person took something ovoid in shape.

Similarly, it seems that there are lawlike generalizations connecting desires for coffee with various predictable sorts of behavior. This accounts for our intuition that the desire for coffee, unlike the ovoid shape of the Prozac pill, has some causal relevance and is not merely epiphenomenal. If a person desires coffee, and coffee is readily available, and the person has no strong reason to avoid coffee, then, *ceteris paribus,* the person will have some coffee. Because of the existence of such humble, commonsense, lawlike generalizations, we can causally explain a person's getting coffee on the grounds that the person desired coffee.

Jerry Fodor has suggested that the following is a sufficient condition for a property to be causally responsible: P is a causally responsible property if P is a property in virtue of which individuals are subsumed by causal laws.[7] Fodor is willing to count *ceteris paribus* laws as genuine causal laws. He admits that for something to be a law, the satisfaction of the antecedent must be nomologically sufficient for the satisfaction of the consequent.[8] This would seem not to hold for *ceteris paribus* laws. But Fodor argues that it does hold for *ceteris paribus* laws when the *ceteris paribus* conditions are satisfied. The presence of a *ceteris paribus* clause in a law signals the presence of some mechanism in virtue of which the satisfaction of the antecedent will bring about the satisfaction of the consequent when that mechanism has not been interfered with. Such mechanisms are presumably physical—so all causally relevant concepts pick out physical mechanisms in some sense. But it doesn't follow that only physical properties (properties mentioned in physical science) are causally relevant. Higher-level properties are causally relevant if such properties occur in lawlike generalizations that back causal explanations.

For example, suppose we explain the fact that Mount Everest has snow and ice near the summit on the grounds that Mount Everest is a tall mountain. Is 'being a tall mountain' a causally relevant property?

One might argue as follows: Being a tall mountain supervenes on various lower-level physical properties such as having an altitude within a certain range, having one of a set of specific geophysical origins, and so on. The fact that Mount Everest has snow and ice near the summit is causally explained by the physical properties that realize Mount Everest's tall-mountainhood, not by its tall-mountainhood. Mount Everest's being a tall mountain is therefore epiphenomenal and causally irrelevant.

Fodor rejects such an argument, giving the following counterargument: Being a tall mountain, despite the fact that it is supervenient, is a genuinely causally relevant property; it is not just epiphenomenal. This is because there are *ceteris paribus* laws linking being a tall mountain with certain effects, such as having snow and ice near the summit. Some physical mechanism guarantees that if M is a tall mountain, and no unusual factors interfere, then M will have snow and ice near the summit. What is true of being a tall mountain is true of being in any particular mental state, according to Fodor. Mental properties enter into *ceteris paribus* laws that can back causal explanations. So, mental properties are truly causally relevant; they are not epiphenomenal.

It would be lovely if we could accept Fodor's argument, but there is a fatal flaw in it. Fodor commits the common error of conflating supervenience with multiple realization.

Fodor's examples of causally relevant 'supervening' properties, which he compares to mental properties, are *not supervenient properties at all*. They are reducible properties that might be identified with their disjunctive physical realization bases. Consider the property of being a tall mountain. There is nothing about that property comparable to the normativity of ethical properties or to the subjectivity of mental properties—nothing that would render the property supervenient as opposed to reducible. 'Tall mountain' has no essential connotation that fails to be captured by 'geophysical structure over 10,000 feet in elevation,' for example. As I have previously stressed, modern notions of property identity (reduction) allow a higher-level property to be identified with a complex disjunctive physical property. Where a given higher-level property reduces to a physical property, no problem about causation arises. What creates the problem in cases of mental causation is that there are *two* properties, neither reducible to the other, and both compete as causes of the same bit of behavior. That is, there are two causal explanations, in vocabularies with irreducibly different connotations, competing as accounts of the same event.

To make this clear, consider again the example of my going into the kitchen to get coffee because I desire coffee. Let us assume that having a subjective desire for coffee is an irreducibly mental property. It supervenes on physical states of brains, but it cannot be identified with the disjunction of physical states that realizes it. (The vocabulary in which we speak of desire, belief, and other subjective states has connotations that would be lost if we attempted to speak in purely neurophysiological terms.) In that case, we have two competing causal explanations of my action: one in physical terms (I performed certain bodily motions because my brain was in such-and-such physical states) and one in mental terms (I fetched coffee because I wanted coffee). Which explanation is correct?

It seems superfluous to acknowledge two causes of the same behavioral event; one cause is enough. But if mental and physical properties are irreducibly distinct, that is, if mentalistic vocabulary cannot be translated without loss of meaning into neurophysiological vocabulary, we have here two putatively complete causal explanations. Methodological principles of parsimony militate in favor of getting rid of one of the causal explanations. Since we have a comparatively clear understanding of how physical properties can be causes and little idea of how subjective properties could be causes *qua* subjective, our tendency is to get rid of the mentalistic explanation. The mental property, as well as whatever *ceteris paribus* laws it may enter into, would seem to be unnecessary in explaining the bodily motions constitutive of my fetching coffee.

Fodor would no doubt point out that we need an explanation in mentalistic terms in order to account for my behavior *described as an action*. If one asks why I went into the kitchen, it is no help to be given a physiological description of the relevant brain states; one wants an explanation that characterizes my behavior as rational—as a response to subjectively perceived states. This is why *ceteris paribus* laws in mental terms exist, Fodor would stress: We require generalizations in such terms in order to make sense of each other's behavior.

But this response does not tell us where mental properties get their presumed causal power. Mental properties are, again, *different properties* than the disjunctive physical properties on which they supervene. (Again, this is just another way of saying the following: Mentalistic vocabulary cannot be replaced with neurophysiological vocabulary without loss of meaning; essential connotations of subjectivity would be lost.) If mental properties enter into their own laws and hence into causal explanations of action, these properties must have causal power. But where does such causal power come from? Fodor's principle, that entering into causal laws is sufficient for possessing genuine causal power, appears disingenuous. Surely, properties enter into laws *because they have causal power,* not the other way around.

In order to get around this problem, Fodor would seemingly have to endorse a principle of the sort Jaegwon Kim has called 'the principle of causal inheritance'.[9] Where M is a particular supervenient mental property and P is a particular subvenient physical property, the principle of causal inheritance is as follows:

> Principle of Causal Inheritance (PCI): If M is instantiated on a given occasion by being realized by P, then the causal powers of *this instance of* M are identical with (perhaps, a subset of) the causal powers of P.

According to Kim, however, a consistent non-reductivist about mental properties must reject PCI; unless the supervening mental property has causal powers *independent of* the causal powers of its physical base, *it is not a genuinely distinct property.* Kim takes it to be common ground that properties are individuated by reference to their causal powers.[10] If mental properties have no unique causal powers of their own, they are not real properties; they are worse than epiphenomena—they don't exist at all.

Kim concludes that a non-reductivist about mental properties must be committed to a spooky sort of 'downward causation': Mental properties, if they are truly distinct from physical properties, must have special causal powers of their own that reach 'down' into the physical world. Unless mental properties have these special causal powers, independent of the causal powers of their physical realization bases, then mental properties must be eliminated as unreal. (Kim's own position, apparently, is that mental properties *are* real but that they are reducible to complex disjunctive physical properties. Kim rejects the central contention of this book, that mental properties are irreducible due to their essential subjective nature.[11])

I, for one, do not wish to endorse spooky downward causation. I believe (as Fodor presumably does) that mental properties inherit their causal powers from the physical properties on which they supervene. What can be done to rescue non-reductive materialism from Kim's argument?

The option I choose is to reject Kim's idea that properties are necessarily individuated by their causal powers. Kim is surely right that most properties are individuated with respect to causal powers, but there are exceptions to the rule. Some properties intrude their way into our ontology not because they have unique, independent causal powers but because they are obvious features of our first-person experience. Subjective (mental) properties, and perhaps evaluative (moral) properties, are examples.[12]

It is important in this discussion to keep in mind the real philosophical issue about mental causation, an issue that unfortunately tends to become obscured when matters are couched in terms of mental properties and the alleged causal relevance of such properties. What must be remembered at all times is the following: What is at issue is whether we can give up our view of ourselves as agents, beings with contentful states who perform actions for consciously apprehended reasons. To admit that "mental properties have no genuine causal power" is the same as admitting that belief/desire explanations of action are never true; it is the same as admitting that we aren't really agents (persons).

Compare this with Kim's claim that mental properties must reduce to physical properties in order to be real. This is the same as claiming the following: If the mentalistic vocabulary has any legitimacy (if it is capable of providing true descriptions and explanations) it must be translatable without loss of meaning into neurophysiological terms.

My own position is twofold: We cannot give up our view of ourselves as agents; we are pragmatically constrained to accept belief/desire explanations of action as (sometimes) true. But it is also true that the mentalistic vocabulary has unique connotations, having to do with subjectivity, that would be lost were we to learn the physical supervenience bases of mental properties and then attempt to speak about ourselves using just neurophysiological vocabulary. The mentalistic vocabulary cannot be replaced without loss of essential meaning.

If I revert to the usual way of setting up the problem of mental causation and accordingly speak of mental properties rather than mentalistic vocabulary, I must put my view in this way: Mental properties are not reducible to physical properties, yet they are genuine features of reality possessing genuine causal power (in that they enter relevantly into true causal explanations). Mental properties have no causal powers independent of the causal powers of the physical properties on which they supervene on particular occasions (the inheritance principle is true) but this lack of independent causal power is not sufficient reason to deny reality to mental properties. No sufficient reason to deny reality to mental properties can be imagined; their reality is manifest, as is their causal power.

If we combine the thesis that mental properties are supervenient subjective aspects of brain states with the inheritance principle, we get, I believe, the true picture of how mental causation works. Mental states are physical states of our brains, and they cause our actions. We experience these states 'from the inside', subjectively. Some of these states come about in such a way, or in such circumstances, that the actions proceeding from them are freely done; others come about in such a way, or in such circumstances, that actions proceeding from them are not freely done. That's all there is to it. Persons who are bothered by this picture are, I suspect, victims of false views regarding the nature of free will.

❧ 9 ❧

Summary, Loose Ends, Conclusions

NOW THAT THIS introduction to the mind-body problem is drawing to a close, it is appropriate to look back and summarize its main arguments and conclusions. Along the way, some peripheral questions that may have occurred to readers will be addressed.

When I reflect on substance dualism, I always think of a song that was popular years ago by Sting (who was then with a rock group called the Police). The song's lyrics, like the lyrics of many songs by the Police, were rather repetitious. The song went: "We are spirits in the material world, are spirits in the material world, are spirits in the material world, are spirits ... "[1] If the arguments in Chapter 1 are sound, Sting was wrong; we are *not* spirits in the material world.

The mind-body problem is that of accounting for the presence of certain beings in the physical world: beings who are conscious selves and rational agents. Many are tempted to suppose that conscious thought and agency must be the products of a non-physical soul or spirit, but I have argued that such substance dualism cannot be rationally maintained in the face of what we have learned from biology and other physical sciences. A human being is a complex physical organism, nothing more. Somehow, selfhood and agency must emerge from the biological functioning of this organism. To suppose that we are souls who will continue to think and act after our bodies die is nothing more than wishful thinking. Serious work on the mind-body problem must begin with materialist assumptions.

Once we abandon the idea that we are spirits inhabiting bodies (ghosts in machines), we are faced with the problem of giving an account of the nature of mental properties. What is it to be in pain? What is it to believe that Santa Fe is the capital of New Mexico?

Many thinkers who have considered this issue have been tempted by reductive physicalist (type identity) theories: theories that identify mental properties with particular physical properties. According to such theories, what it is to be in pain is to be in a certain type of brain state; likewise, what it is to believe that Santa Fe is the capital of New Mexico is to be in a certain type of brain state. The brain state types hypothesized as being identical to mental state types might be very complex disjunctions of different physical states; reductive physicalism allows for so-called multiple realization of mental state types.

Others have been tempted to identify mental properties with behavioral properties. This approach, known as logical behaviorism, identifies pain and the belief that Santa Fe is the capital of New Mexico with particular sets of behavior dispositions.

Another popular theory regarding the nature of mental properties has been functionalism. Functionalism is an extension of logical behaviorism; functionalists identify mental properties with functional properties. A functional property is the property of playing a certain role in a system: being caused in certain typical ways, interacting with other states of the system in certain ways, and producing specified outputs under specified circumstances. Functionalism is often married to the computer model of the mind to yield computational theories of mind. Computationalists consider mental states to be analogous to the program states of a computer.

Type identity theory, logical behaviorism, and functionalism all fall afoul of the same difficulty. These theories are supposed to tell us what mental properties *are* in non-mental terms; they are supposed to give us a *reduction* of mental properties to some other, more 'scientifically respectable' properties. But, it seems, no account of the nature of mental properties in non-mental terms can be given. To be in a certain mental state is, essentially, to be in a certain *subjective* state. The essence of pain is to hurt; the essence of believing that Santa Fe is the capital of New Mexico is having direct cognitive awareness of a certain bit of information. No account of the nature of such essentially subjective properties in objective terms can possibly succeed.

As an alternative to the idea that mental properties reduce to physical, behavioral, or functional properties, I recommended the thesis that mental properties supervene on physical properties. This means that every individual mental state is some physical state (mental states are realized in physical states), but still, the property of being in a given type of mental state cannot be identified with any physical property. If two states are alike physically, they must realize the same mental state; there can be no difference in mental states without some difference in physical states. Mental properties are determined by physical properties but are not identifiable with physical properties.

I suggested that mental properties supervene on physical properties in the same way moral properties have been suggested to supervene on physical properties. A moral property, such as wrongness, is always realized in some physical state of affairs or other. And if some state of affairs is wrong, a descriptively exactly similar state of affairs must also be wrong. Wrongness itself, however, cannot be identified with the vast disjunction of physical features that realize it. Wrongness as a property contains an evaluative element that fails to be captured by any descriptive account of states of affairs. Similarly, mental properties have subjective elements (analogous to the evaluative elements of moral properties) that cannot be captured by any objective description of a mental property's physical base.

A certain reductionist/physicalist ideology, however, asserts that all properties entering into scientifically respectable descriptions and explanations must reduce to physical properties. If any property fails to so reduce, that property must be eliminated, along with any descriptions and explanations into which it enters. This ideology is the main driving force behind eliminative materialism, the thesis that mental properties will be thrown out as outmoded constructs of a false folk theory.

I contended that the reductionist/physicalist ideology is self-defeating, given the strong probability that mental properties will not reduce to physical properties (because of their essentially subjective nature). Even eliminative materialists take themselves to be agents, beings who act rationally (do things for reasons). The possibility that mental properties and their associated causal explanations of action could be eliminated cannot seriously be maintained by anyone who takes himself to be an agent. Like it or not, the reductionist/physicalist is stuck with mental properties and mentalistic explanations of behavior.

The failure of both reduction and elimination with regard to mental properties forces us to consider property dualist (non-reductive materialist) mind-body theories. Property dualists accept that mental properties will not reduce to any other sort of property, but they also accept that mental properties are real features of the world that may enter into legitimate descriptions and explanations.

Two influential versions of non-reductive materialism are due to Donald Davidson and Daniel C. Dennett. But there are flaws in both of these theories. Davidson wants to maintain both that mental properties supervene on (are determined by) physical properties and that mental properties are anomalous (not predictable on the basis of physical law); it seems he can't have it both ways. Dennett wants to maintain both that mental properties are *abstracta,* attributed to systems by outside observers for predictive purposes, and that mental properties can enter into causal explanations of action. It is hard to understand how an *abstractum* could play any genuine causal role.

Davidson's and Dennett's theories both lean toward the idea that mental properties are primarily constructs attributed to agents from outside, from the third-person point of view; such attribution is constrained by holistic and normative principles. I argued that this flies in the face of the most obvious fact of all about mental states: They are essentially subjective states, apprehended introspectively from the first-person point of view. Because we know our mental states directly, by acquaintance, they cannot be third-person constructs.

A satisfactory version of non-reductive materialism would acknowledge the first-person character of mental states. It would embrace the idea that subjective mental properties supervene locally on physical properties of brains. I argued that objections to the notion that mental content is subjectively known can be met; I also argued that a popular objection to the thesis that content is locally supervenient on brain states is mistaken.

I argued that externalism about mental content rests upon some false assumptions, such as the assumption that the contents of our beliefs are always accurately captured by the that-clauses language uses to characterize such contents. Language may be more or less successful in capturing the truth-conditions of thoughts. The subjective truth-conditions of thoughts constitute mental content; such content is 'in the head'.

Finally, I considered the problem of mental causation. Mental causation poses a major problem for substance dualists. Physical substance is supposed to be extended in space; mental substance is supposed to be non-extended. How can two substances, one extended and the other not, interact causally? This was a deep puzzle for philosophers of the seventeenth and eighteenth centuries, but our materialist metaphysics allows us to sidestep it. The problem of mental causation arises in a new form, however, within non-reductive materialism.

We take it for granted that causal relations fall under causal laws. The most basic causal laws connect physical properties with other physical properties. Causal explanations that make use of higher-level, non-physicalistic vocabulary can usually be reduced to causal explanations in physical terms by identifying the properties expressed by the higher-level terms with physical properties. For example, suppose we explain why a particular substance splashes on some occasion on the grounds that it is liquid. Liquidity can be reduced to some physical property (perhaps a single structural property or perhaps a disjunction of many different physical properties in different liquids). Therefore, our causal explanation in terms of liquidity can be reduced to a causal explanation in physical terms, backed by a physical causal law.

Causal explanations of action that make reference to mental properties, however, cannot be reduced to causal explanations in physical terms. Mental properties, because of their essential subjectivity, cannot be identified with their physical bases. This means that actions, *qua* actions, do not fall under physical causal laws. It may appear that on any given occasion when a person seems to perform an action for a reason, all the real causal work is being done by the physical properties of the person's brain. Mental properties, while realized in physical properties, cannot be identified with physical properties and accordingly seem to be just 'hanging around'. If mental properties do no causal work, epiphenomenalism is true; we are, in T. H. Huxley's words, 'conscious automata', not genuine agents.

I argued that the problem of mental causation can be made to vanish if we endorse an 'inheritance principle' according to which mental properties inherit the causal powers of the physical states on which they supervene on given occasions. This means that mental properties have no causal power independent of the causal power of their underlying physical base properties, but that should not bother us. Mental properties are still real. In most cases, we take a given property to be real only if that property has independent causal powers. But mental properties are an exception: We take mental properties to be real because their reality is forced on us; we cannot be unaware of our own awareness.

Some readers will no doubt be dissatisfied with my account of mental causation. How, it will be asked, does my account differ from epiphenomenalism? The answer is simple. According to epiphenomenalism, mental properties have no causal powers at all. According to my view, mental properties have the same causal powers as the physical states that realize them on particular occasions.

It is true that on my account mental properties don't add anything to the physical causal nexus. I believe that our mental states are just physical states, causally dependent on other physical states and causing other physical states in virtue of their physical properties. We experience these states from within, as conscious selves. We are genuine agents and not Huxleyan automata because often our mental states and actions come about in such a way, and under such circumstances, that it is correct to describe us as free. This compatibilist view of the nature of free will is counterintuitive to many persons, at least at first, but on reflection it can come to seem obviously true. At any rate, it is the only conception of freedom that sits well with a naturalistic worldview.

My approving appeal to a naturalistic worldview may be another factor that arouses the ire of some readers. (Naturalism, roughly, is the thesis that whatever can be explained in terms acceptable to physical science, without appeal to gods or spirits, should be so explained.) What, it will be asked, is my ultimate motivation for being a naturalist? My dismissal of substance dualism may seem to proceed from an unthinking acceptance of naturalism, and I may be called upon to justify my reliance on that philosophical orientation.

Naturalism has many aspects, both ontological and methodological; I cannot here attempt either a precise definition of naturalism or a detailed justification of it. But I will say this much: I take naturalism to be motivated primarily by its past success. Ever since human beings stopped trying to explain things in terms of gods and spirits and started trying to explain things scientifically, our predictions have become much more accurate and our explanations have become much more powerful. Accordingly, we have been able to manipulate the environment successfully; we have been able to make things that work. We have gone from being ignorant victims of processes we did not understand to being knowledgeable agents, able to pursue our ends with power. I take this successful track record to suggest that naturalism is a good idea.

As I stressed in Chapter 1, I do not wish my naturalism to be confused with scientism. Not all questions are appropriately addressed by scientific methods; hence, science can't solve all our problems. I do, however, take the great success of science and other rational methods to justify the following: The questions science can answer, science should answer, and what science can't answer should be addressed rationally, in terms acceptable to science.

One last loose end begs to be addressed. I have suggested the supervenience of mental properties on physical properties as a solution to the mind-body problem. But does the supervenience thesis really explain anything? It may be objected that the supervenience thesis, far from being a solution to the mind-body problem, is just an elaborate restatement of the problem.

Recall the mind-body problem in its most naive form: Why are we conscious selves? We are, after all, just complex blobs of physical matter. Why should we be aware of ourselves and of our world? Why should we have thoughts, feelings, desires, and intentions? Why should we be capable of performing actions for reasons? What makes any of these wondrous facts true? It may be said with some justification that to be told mentality supervenes on the brain is not very illuminating or helpful.

The mind-brain supervenience thesis, like most philosophical theories, is really more a clarification of the problem than it is a solution to the problem. But is that so bad? What *would* qualify as a genuine solution to the mind-body problem? Could *science,* perhaps, solve the mind-body problem?

Science may someday be able to tell us all the physical facts about what goes on in our brains. But will that tell us why consciousness emerges from those physical processes? No.

The mind-body problem is not a scientific problem. It is a philosophical problem, one of those eternal puzzles that strikes human beings as requiring an answer yet cannot be addressed by empirical methodology. It is typical of philosophical problems that no answer that is proposed seems quite satisfying or definitive, yet the rational process of coming to an ever deeper understanding of a philosophical problem is profoundly seductive. This process tells us much about our own nature and limitations as well as telling us about our world. As Bertrand Russell put it, in words more eloquent than I could ever write:

> Philosophy is to be studied, not for the sake of any definite answers to its questions, since no definite answers can, as a rule, be known to be true; but rather

for the sake of the questions themselves; because these questions enlarge our conception of what is possible, enrich our intellectual imagination and diminish the dogmatic assurance which closes the mind against speculation; but above all because, through the greatness of the universe which philosophy contemplates, the mind also is rendered great, and becomes capable of that union with the universe which constitutes its highest good.[2]

Notes

Chapter 1

1. Rene Descartes, *Meditations on First Philosophy*, trans. by Donald A. Cress (Indianapolis: Hackett Publishing Co., 1979). The passages quoted are from Meditation Six.

2. The main argument that God exists and is not a deceiver is in Meditation Three. Descartes also offers an argument for the existence of God in Meditation Five.

3. In Meditation Four, Descartes argues that the 'faculty of judgment' given to him by God is accurate when properly used. By this 'faculty of judgment' Descartes means the ability to make judgments, that is, to judge that something is so. There is a circularity (perhaps a fatal circularity) in Descartes's reasoning. Descartes accepts that God exists on the grounds that his argument for the existence of God is so 'clear and distinct' it cannot be doubted; then he argues that we cannot doubt the conclusions of our 'clear and distinct' arguments on the grounds that God exists and is not a deceiver. The way out of this Cartesian circle is not clear.

4. Plato, *Meno*, trans. by G.M.A. Grube (Indianapolis: Hackett Publishing Co., 1976), reprinted in Steven M. Cahn, ed., *Classics of Western Philosophy*, 3d ed. (Indianapolis: Hackett Publishing Co., 1977).

5. For a selection of papers covering all positions on the problem of free will and determinism, see Gary Watson, *Free Will* (Oxford: Oxford University Press, 1982).

6. See generally Joel Feinberg, "Action and Responsibility," and P. J. Fitzgerald, "Voluntary and Involuntary Acts," in Alan R. White, ed., *The Philosophy of Action* (Oxford: Oxford University Press, 1968).

Chapter 2

1. It is common for philosophers to assert that only propositional attitudes, not qualitative states, have content. I object to this usage, for the reason given in the text: Qualia, like the propositional contents of beliefs and desires, are part of the subjective, inner lives of persons. Those who reserve 'content' for propositional attitudes alone have in mind intentional content, which (I believe) is only one sort of subjective content.

2. The word 'intension' is roughly synonymous with such terms as 'sense', 'conceptual meaning', and 'connotation'. The word 'extension' is roughly synonymous with such terms as 'reference' and 'denotation'. Both singular terms (terms that refer to one particular individual) and general terms (kind terms) possess intension and extension. For example, the singular term 'the moon' has a particular intension or sense; it conjures up particular standard associations and images in the mind of any competent user of the term. 'The moon' also has a particular extension or denotation; it refers to a

certain large physical object in orbit around the earth. Likewise, the general term 'table' has an intension and an extension. The intension of 'table' is the standard conceptual meaning of the word; the extension of 'table' is all the objects that are tables. The intension/extension distinction (sense/reference distinction) is famously discussed by German logician Gottlob Frege in "On Sense and Nominatum," reprinted in A. P. Martinich, ed., *The Philosophy of Language*, 2d ed. (New York: Oxford University Press, 1990).

3. The alleged special properties of natural kind concepts have been explored by Saul Kripke and Hilary Putnam. See Kripke, *Naming and Necessity* (Cambridge: Cambridge University Press, 1972); Putnam, "Meaning and Reference," *Journal of Philosophy* 70 (1973), pp. 699–711.

4. For example, see Paul Churchland, "Eliminative Materialism and Propositional Attitudes," *Journal of Philosophy* 78 (1981), pp. 67–90. See also Jaegwon Kim, "Multiple Realization and the Metaphysics of Reduction," *Philosophy and Phenomenological Research* 52, no. 1 (1992), pp. 1–26.

5. Some materialists may object to this usage and prefer the more precise claim that having an appropriately functioning brain is sufficient for having the set of mental capacities we call a mind. That a mind is, properly speaking, a set of capacities for intelligent behavior, and not a physical organ, is the view of Anthony Kenny. See Kenny, *The Metaphysics of Mind* (Oxford: Clarendon Press, 1989).

6. Those who dissent from token materialism may do so for various reasons, but one such reason is *externalism* about the content of propositional attitudes. Externalists such as Tyler Burge think that a person and his or her token states of the moment could exist in a counterfactual situation in which that person's mental contents would be different because of the different sociolinguistic environment. See the discussion of content externalism in Chapter 7 and the works by Burge and others cited in that chapter. (Thanks here are due to Ned Block for reminding me that there is no consensus on the truth of token materialism.)

7. U. T. Place, "Is Consciousness a Brain Process?" *British Journal of Psychology* 47 (1956), pp. 44–50; J.J.C. Smart, "Sensations and Brain Processes," *Philosophical Review* 68 (1959), pp. 141–156; Herbert Feigl, "The 'Mental' and the 'Physical'," *Minnesota Studies in the Philosophy of Science*, Vol. 2 (Minneapolis: University of Minnesota Press, 1958), pp. 474–485.

8. See Saul Kripke, *Naming and Necessity* (Cambridge: Cambridge University Press, 1972).

9. This is a bit of an oversimplification. It is not so clear that water is identical with H_2O without qualification. Water vapor is H_2O but not water; ice is H_2O but not water; seawater is water but not pure H_2O; a single water molecule is H_2O but not water; heavy water is water but is not H_2O, and so on. I am ignoring such qualifications for the sake of making a point.

10. See Kripke, *Naming and Necessity*.

11. The old, outmoded conception of property reduction is that of Ernest Nagel. See Nagel, *The Structure of Science* (New York: Harcourt, Brace, and World, 1961).

12. See Patricia Churchland, "Reductionism and Antireductionism in Functionalist Theories of Mind," in Brian Beakley and Peter Ludlow, eds., *The Philosophy of Mind: Classical Problems, Contemporary Issues* (Cambridge: MIT Press, 1992), pp. 59–67.

13. See Jaegwon Kim, "Multiple Realization and the Metaphysics of Reduction," *Philosophy and Phenomenological Research* 52, no. 1 (March 1992), pp. 1–26.

14. Saul Kripke, "Identity and Necessity," in Brian Beakley and Peter Ludlow, eds., *The Philosophy of Mind: Classical Problems, Contemporary Issues* (Cambridge: MIT Press, 1992), pp. 41–45.

15. See R. M. Hare, *The Language of Morals* (Oxford: Clarendon Press, 1952), ch. 9, p. 145 (this passage marks the first time 'supervenience' was used in a philosophical context). See also G. E. Moore, "The Conception of Intrinsic Value," in G. E. Moore, *Philosophical Studies* (Paterson, N. J.: Littlefield, Adams, and Co., 1959), p. 261.

16. Gilbert Ryle, *The Concept of Mind* (New York: Barnes and Noble, 1949).

17. It is ironic that this is often taken to be a criticism of Ryle, since Ryle explicitly admits it. See Ryle, *The Concept of Mind*, ch. 5. It appears that many of the critics of logical behaviorism have never actually read Ryle and so do not realize how similar Rylean logical behaviorism is to its successor, functionalism.

18. See Ned Block, "The Computer Model of the Mind," in D. Osherson and E. E. Smith, eds., *An Invitation to Cognitive Science*, Vol. 3 (Cambridge: MIT Press, 1990).

19. See Alan Turing, "Computing Machinery and Intelligence," *Mind* 59 (1950), pp. 433–460.

20. Block, "The Computer Model of the Mind," pp. 249–250.

21. See J. Weizenbaum, *Computer Power and Human Reason* (San Francisco: W. H. Freeman, 1976). Discussion of ELIZA occurs on pp. 188–191.

22. Block, "The Computer Model of the Mind," p. 250.

Chapter 3

1. David Lewis, "Psychological and Theoretical Identification," *Australasian Journal of Philosophy* 50 (1972), pp. 249–258; "How to Define Theoretical Terms," in David Lewis, *Philosophical Papers*, Vol. 1 (New York: Oxford University Press, 1983), pp. 78–95.

2. Hilary Putnam, "The Nature of Mental States," in Brian Beakley and Peter Ludlow, eds., *The Philosophy of Mind: Classical Problems, Contemporary Issues* (Cambridge: MIT Press, 1992), pp. 51–58.

3. William Lycan, "Towards a Homuncular Theory of Believing," *Cognition and Brain Theory* 4 (1981), pp. 139–159; "Form, Function, and Feel," *Journal of Philosophy* 78 (1981), pp. 24–50; *Consciousness* (Cambridge: MIT Press, 1987).

4. Kim Sterelny, *The Representational Theory of Mind: An Introduction* (Cambridge: Basil Blackwell, 1991).

5. Robert Cummins, "Functional Analysis," *Journal of Philosophy* 72 (1975), pp. 741–765.

6. Daniel C. Dennett, "Why the Law of Effect Will Not Go Away," *Journal of the Theory of Social Behavior* 5 (1974), pp. 169–187.

7. Jerry Fodor, "The Appeal to Tacit Knowledge in Psychological Explanation," *Journal of Philosophy* 65 (1968), pp. 627–640.

8. Putnam, "The Nature of Mental States," in Beakley and Ludlow, eds., *The Philosophy of Mind*, pp. 51–58.

9. Putnam, "Philosophy and Our Mental Life," in Beakley and Ludlow, eds., *The Philosophy of Mind*, pp. 91–99.

10. Putnam, *Representation and Reality* (Cambridge: MIT Press, 1988).

11. My Turing gumball machine is based on a Turing Coke machine utilized by Ned Block in "Troubles with Functionalism," in Beakley and Ludlow, eds., *The Philosophy of Mind,* pp. 69–90, at p. 72. Although gumball machines are seldom known to give change, I have changed the Coke machine to a gumball machine, due to the inflated price of Cokes these days. Thanks to Ned Block for his permission to use the idea.

12. In Figure 3.2 I have assumed that an input of morphine will cause a person to go from a state of pain into a state of non-pain. This is controversial. Readers have suggested to me that when one receives morphine for pain, one remains in pain; one "just doesn't give a damn." I don't wish to take a position on this. Figure 3.2 is intended as an illustration of part of a hypothetical Turing machine table, not as a statement regarding the true effect of morphine.

13. Putnam, "Philosophy and Our Mental Life," in Beakley and Ludlow, eds., *The Philosophy of Mind,* pp. 91–99.

14. Ned Block (in personal correspondence) suggests that what I am calling homuncular functionalism is just a species of what he calls *psychofunctionalism,* that is, Lewis-style functionalism where the Ramsified theory is a scientific psychological theory.

15. The example given is based on Lycan, "Towards a Homuncular Theory of Believing," pp. 33–34, as reported in Sterelny, *The Representational Theory of Mind,* p. 16.

16. Sterelny, *The Representational Theory of Mind,* p. 13.

17. Jerry Fodor, *The Language of Thought* (New York: Thomas Y. Crowell Co., reprinted by Harvard University Press, 1979).

18. Fodor has speculated in several works as to just how internal representations might get their meaning (content) via causal relations with what they represent. See Jerry Fodor, *Psychosemantics: The Problem of Meaning in the Philosophy of Mind* (Cambridge: MIT Press, 1987); *A Theory of Content and Other Essays* (Cambridge: MIT Press, 1990).

19. John Searle, "Minds, Brains, and Programs," *Behavioral and Brain Sciences* 3, (1980) pp. 417–457.

20. See John Searle, *The Rediscovery of the Mind* (Cambridge: MIT Press, 1992).

21. See Ned Block, "The Computer Model of the Mind," ch. 3 of D. Osherson and E. E. Smith, eds., *An Invitation to Cognitive Science,* Vol. 3 (Cambridge: MIT Press, 1990), pp. 284–286.

22. See Searle, *The Rediscovery of the Mind.*

23. Searle, *The Rediscovery of the Mind,* Ch. 9.

24. Examples of philosophers who pursue the causal representationalist strategy are Jerry Fodor and Fred Dretske. See Fodor, *Psychosemantics* and *A Theory of Content and Other Essays;* Dretske, *Knowledge and the Flow of Information* (Cambridge: MIT Press, 1981), and *Explaining Behavior: Reasons in a World of Causes* (Cambridge: MIT Press, 1988).

25. See Ruth Millikan, *Language, Thought, and Other Biological Categories* (Cambridge: MIT Press, 1984).

26. Searle, *The Rediscovery of the Mind,* p. 50.

Chapter 4

1. Richard Rorty, "In Defense of Eliminative Materialism," *Review of Metaphysics* 24 (1970), pp. 112–121.

2. Paul Feyerabend, "Materialism and the Mind-Body Problem," *Review of Metaphysics* 17 (1963), pp. 49–66.

3. Paul Churchland, "Eliminative Materialism and Propositional Attitudes," *Journal of Philosophy* 78 (1981), pp. 67–90.

4. Stephen Stich, *From Folk Psychology to Cognitive Science: The Case Against Belief* (Cambridge: MIT Press, 1983).

5. Michael Devitt and Kim Sterelny, *Language and Reality: An Introduction to the Philosophy of Language* (Cambridge: MIT Press, 1987).

6. Michael McCloskey, "Intuitive Physics," *Scientific American* 248/4 (1983), pp. 122–130; Michael McCloskey, Alfonso Caramazza, and Bert Green, "Curvilinear Motion in the Absence of External Forces: Naive Beliefs About the Motion of Objects," *Science* 210/4474 (1980), pp. 1139–1141. Both papers are cited in Patricia Churchland, *Neurophilosophy: Toward a Unified Science of the Mind-Brain* (Cambridge: MIT Press, 1986).

7. Daniel C. Dennett, *The Intentional Stance* (Cambridge: MIT Press, 1987), pp. 7–8.

8. I believe that John Searle's notion of a 'background of intentionality' provides a plausible account of the nature of the unarticulated know-how that has often been mistakenly called 'folk theory'. See John Searle, *Intentionality* (Cambridge: Cambridge University Press, 1983), ch. 5.

9. For an example of this type of argument, see Paul Churchland, "Eliminative Materialism and Propositional Attitudes," *Journal of Philosophy* 78 (1981), pp. 67–90, at p. 73.

10. On deductive-nomological explanation and its relation to reduction, see Patricia Churchland, *Neurophilosophy*; see also Ernest Nagel, *The Structure of Science* (New York: Harcourt, Brace, and World, 1961); Nicholas Rescher, *Scientific Explanation* (New York: Free Press, 1970); Carl G. Hempel, *Aspects of Scientific Explanation* (New York: Free Press, 1965).

11. Ernest Nagel, *The Structure of Science* (New York: Harcourt, Brace, and World, 1961).

12. For example, see C. A. Hooker, "Towards a General Theory of Reduction," Parts 1, 2, and 3, *Dialogue* 20 (1981), pp. 38–59, 201–236, 496–529.

13. See Patricia Churchland, "Reductionism and Antireductionism in Functionalist Theories of Mind," in Brian Beakley and Peter Ludlow, eds., *The Philosophy of Mind: Classical Problems, Contemporary Issues* (Cambridge: MIT Press, 1992), pp. 59–67.

14. See Paul Churchland, *A Neurocomputational Perspective: The Nature of Mind and the Structure of Science* (Cambridge: MIT Press, 1989), ch. 3.

15. The view that reasons bear causal relations, as well as logical/rational relations, to actions, is defended by Donald Davidson. See Davidson, "Actions, Reasons, and Causes," in Donald Davidson, *Essays on Actions and Events* (Oxford: Clarendon Press, 1980), pp. 3–19. Davidson's paper established the causal view of reasons as the predominant view, in opposition to the previously predominant idea that reasons

could not bear causal relations to action. For a defense of the latter idea, see A. I. Melden, *Free Action* (London: Routledge and Kegan Paul, 1961).

16. Stich, *From Folk Psychology to Cognitive Science.*

17. Hilary Putnam, "Meaning and Reference," *Journal of Philosophy* 70 (1973), pp. 699–711; Tyler Burge, "Individualism and the Mental," in P. French, T. Uehling, and H. Wettstein, eds., *Midwest Studies in Philosophy,* Vol. 5 (Minneapolis: University of Minnesota Press, 1979), pp. 73–122.

18. Hilary Putnam, *Representation and Reality* (Cambridge: MIT Press, 1988).

19. Putnam, *Representation and Reality,* pp. 83–84.

20. Jerry Fodor seems to believe that legitimate causal-explanatory notions must be vindicated by inclusion in some scientific theory. He writes: "Holding onto the attitudes—vindicating commonsense psychology—means showing how you could have (or, at a minimum, showing *that* you could have) a respectable science whose ontology explicitly acknowledges states that exhibit the properties that common sense attributes to the attitudes." Fodor, *Psychosemantics: The Problem of Meaning in the Philosophy of Mind* (Cambridge: MIT Press, 1987), p. 10.

21. Terence Horgan and James Woodward, "Folk Psychology Is Here to Stay," *Philosophical Review* 94 (1985), pp. 197–226.

Chapter 5

1. I call this argument 'the argument that commonsense psychology could not conceivably prove false', but this title is slightly misleading. It is not so much that commonsense psychology could not conceivably be false, for there is no difficulty in imagining a world in which nothing has any mental states, but that there is no way *we,* in our world, can understand how we could find out that commonsense psychology is false.

2. Immanuel Kant, in his *Critique of Pure Reason* and *Prolegomena to Any Future Metaphysics,* uses what he calls a 'transcendental deduction' to show that there are innate human concepts that structure experience. In general, a transcendental argument attempts to show that something must be the case because that something is a necessary precondition of something everybody accepts to be the case.

3. Jerry Fodor, *Psychosemantics: The Problem of Meaning in the Philosophy of Mind* (Cambridge: MIT Press, 1987), pp. 9–10.

4. Bertrand Russell, "Descriptions," reprinted in A. P. Martinich, ed., *The Philosophy of Language,* 1st ed. (New York: Oxford University Press, 1985), pp. 213–219. The passage quoted occurs at p. 214.

5. This example is due to Stephen Stich. See Stich, *From Folk Psychology to Cognitive Science: The Case Against Belief* (Cambridge: MIT Press, 1983), p. 27.

6. Paul Churchland, "Eliminative Materialism and Propositional Attitudes," *Journal of Philosophy* 78 (1981), pp. 67–90, at p. 70.

7. Richard E. Nisbett and Timothy D. Wilson, "Telling More Than We Can Know: Verbal Reports on Mental Processes," *Psychological Review* 84 (1977), pp. 231–259.

8. Patricia Churchland, *Neurophilosophy: Toward a Unified Science of the Mind-Brain* (Cambridge: MIT Press, 1986), p. 309.

9. Colin McGinn, Review of Patricia Churchland, *Neurophilosophy. Times Literary Supplement,* Feb. 6, 1987.

10. Terence Horgan and James Woodward, "Folk Psychology Is Here to Stay," *Philosophical Review* 94 (1985), pp. 197–226; Stephen Schiffer, "Physicalism," *Philosophical Perspectives* 4 (1990), pp. 153–185.

11. Paul Churchland, "Eliminative Materialism and Propositional Attitudes," at p. 89.

12. Lynne Rudder Baker, *Saving Belief* (Princeton: Princeton University Press, 1987), ch. 7.

13. Thanks to Doug Krueger for his help in clarifying my understanding of this famous anecdote.

14. Hilary Putnam, *Representation and Reality* (Cambridge: MIT Press, 1988), ch. 4.

15. Putnam argues that, contrary to popular belief, neither Alfred Tarski's 'semantic conception of truth' nor the 'disquotational' or 'redundancy' theory of truth successfully reduces the commonsense notion of truth to any more naturalistically respectable notion. Putnam, *Representation and Reality*, pp. 60–90.

16. Putnam, *Representation and Reality*, pp. 70–71.

17. Stich, *From Folk Psychology to Cognitive Science*.

18. Zenon Pylyshyn, *Computation and Cognition* (Cambridge: MIT Press, 1984), ch. 1.

19. I would like to thank Rob Cummins for helping me to formulate my version of this argument.

20. Here, by 'behaviorism,' I do not mean the logical behaviorism discussed in Chapter 2. I mean the (now defunct) behaviorist program in psychology, which adopted a methodology according to which non–publicly observable phenomena, such as mental states, were not allowed to figure in explanations of rational action. Rational actions were explained by reference to external stimuli alone.

21. It is also true, I believe, that we can see the system as rational only if the system consciously understands the encoded meaning of the internal symbols. The internal symbols must mean something to the system (organism) itself, not just to an outside interpreter; the symbols must possess intrinsic intentionality. Here I agree with John Searle and disagree with Daniel Dennett. See Searle, *Intentionality* (Cambridge: Cambridge University Press, 1983); Daniel C. Dennett, *The Intentional Stance* (Cambridge: MIT Press, 1987), pp. 287–288.

Chapter 6

1. Donald Davidson, "Mental Events," in Donald Davidson, *Essays on Actions and Events* (Oxford: Clarendon Press, 1980), pp. 207–227.

2. Davidson, "Mental Events," p. 207.

3. For much of my exposition of Davidson's general philosophical position, I am indebted to Simon Evnine, whose remarkably clear and understandable book on Davidson is extremely helpful. See Simon Evnine, *Donald Davidson* (Stanford: Stanford University Press, 1991).

4. Davidson, "Mental Events," pp. 209–210.

5. Davidson, "Mental Events," p. 208.

6. Davidson, "Mental Events," p. 214. Note that Davidson's two characterizations of supervenience are not equivalent. The second is not entailed by the first unless we add that every mental event is a physical event, but that thesis, token identity, is sufficient by itself for the second version of supervenience. Likewise, the second version does not entail the first, for it is compatible with every mental event being a physical event that a token of a given physical event type is identical with a mental event while another token of that physical event type is not identical with a token of any mental event type.

7. Davidson, "Mental Events," p. 215.

8. See Evnine, *Donald Davidson,* p. 7.

9. Evnine, *Donald Davidson,* pp. 17–18.

10. Davidson, "Mental Events," p. 214.

11. The situation is a bit more complicated than I have made it seem in the text. Jaegwon Kim has distinguished two varieties of supervenience: strong supervenience (strong S) and weak supervenience (weak S). Kim, "Concepts of Supervenience," *Philosophy and Phenomenological Research* 45 (1984), pp. 153–176. Only strong S is incompatible with mental anomaly. Davidson, at one point, explicitly stated that his notion of supervenience was weak S, thus avoiding the sort of objection I raise in the text. See Davidson, "Reply to Essays X–XII," in Bruce Vermazen and Merrill Hintikka, eds., *Essays on Davidson: Actions and Events* (Oxford: Oxford University Press, 1985). Kim, however, has pointed out that weak S does not guarantee determination of all properties by physical properties, and Davidson sometimes seems to want to endorse such determination. See Kim, "Concepts of Supervenience," at pp. 162–163. Davidson's first formulation of supervenience in "Mental Events" at least seems to involve determination of mental properties by physical properties, which would make this a formulation of strong S rather than weak S.

12. See Davidson, "Actions, Reasons, and Causes," in Davidson, *Essays on Actions and Events,* pp. 3–19.

13. Daniel C. Dennett, *The Intentional Stance* (Cambridge: MIT Press, 1987).

14. Dennett, *The Intentional Stance,* p. 72.

15. Dennett, *The Intentional Stance,* p. 73. This term, 'true with a grain of salt', is odd. It is natural to regard being true as akin to being pregnant; either a claim is true or it is not. Anyone who claims, as Dennett does, to have a notion of truth susceptible of degrees perhaps owes an account of that notion of truth.

16. Dennett, *The Intentional Stance,* p. 234.

17. Dennett, *The Intentional Stance,* p. 57.

18. Dennett, *The Intentional Stance,* p. 58.

19. Dennett, *The Intentional Stance,* p. 29.

20. There are similarities between Dennett's views on the indeterminacy of propositional attitude sets and W.V.O. Quine's views about the indeterminacy of translation. See W.V.O. Quine, *Word and Object* (Cambridge: MIT Press, 1960), ch. 2. According to Quine, although it may always be possible to provide more than one 'translation manual' for a given language, and although these manuals may be straightforwardly incompatible, there is no further fact of the matter as to which is correct. This view is vulnerable to a certain sort of objection: Surely there is a determinate fact of the matter as to what a person means, accessible to the person from his or her subjective point of view. See John Searle, "Indeterminacy, Empiricism, and the First Person," *Journal of*

Philosophy 84/3 (1987), pp. 123–146. Dennett's view on the nature of mental states is subject to a similar objection: Surely there is a determinate fact of the matter as to what set of beliefs and desires a person really accepts, accessible to that person from his or her subjective viewpoint.

21. Dennett, *The Intentional Stance,* p. 235.

22. Dennett, *The Intentional Stance,* p. 265.

23. Quine, *Word and Object* (Cambridge: MIT Press, 1960), ch. 2.

24. Davidson is somewhat inconsistent. Does he see mental events primarily as constructs attributed from outside, from the third-person point of view, or does he see mental events primarily as real state tokens, physically present in people's brains? Davidson's stress on holism and normativity indicates that the third-person point of view is probably primary for Davidson, though the other viewpoint is also undeniably present in his writings.

Chapter 7

1. Thanks are due to Robert Audi for this point.

2. Hilary Putnam, "Brains in a Vat," in Hilary Putnam, *Reason, Truth, and History* (Cambridge: Cambridge University Press, 1981), pp. 1–21.

3. See Brian Loar, "Subjective Intentionality," *Philosophical Topics* 15, no. 1 (1987), pp. 89–124; see also Frank Jackson and Philip Pettit, "Some Content Is Narrow," in John Heil and Alfred Mele, eds., *Mental Causation* (Oxford: Clarendon Press, 1993), pp. 259–282.

4. See Hilary Putnam, "Meaning and Reference," *Journal of Philosophy* 70 (1973), pp. 699–711, and "The Meaning of 'Meaning'," in Hilary Putnam, *Mind, Language, and Reality: Philosophical Papers,* Vol. 2 (New York: Cambridge University Press, 1975), pp. 215–271; Tyler Burge, "Individualism and the Mental," in P. French, T. Uehling, and H. Wettstein, *Midwest Studies in Philosophy,* Vol. 5 (Minneapolis: University of Minnesota Press, 1979), pp. 73–121, and "Individualism and Psychology," *Philosophical Review* 95 (1986), pp. 3–46; Stephen Stich, *From Folk Psychology to Cognitive Science: The Case Against Belief* (Cambridge: MIT Press, 1983).

5. It is really not plausible that my twin and I could be in identical physical states given the fact that so much of the human body is composed of water. But this is not crucial to the effectiveness of the thought-experiment. I have my dialogue characters mention this issue in the last section of the present chapter.

6. Putnam, "Meaning and Reference," p. 704.

7. See Donald Davidson, "Actions, Reasons, and Causes," in Donald Davidson, *Essays on Actions and Events* (Oxford: Clarendon Press, 1980), pp. 3–19. For the contrary view, that propositional attitudes rationalize action without causally explaining it, see A. I. Melden, *Free Action* (London: Routledge and Kegan Paul, 1961).

8. See Robert Audi, "Dispositional Beliefs and Dispositions to Believe," forthcoming in *Nous.*

9. This example of a putative belief (really, a disposition to believe) is due to Stephen Stich. See Stich, *From Folk Psychology to Cognitive Science: The Case Against Belief* (Cambridge: MIT Press, 1983).

10. The "sage in New Jersey" is Jerry Fodor. See Fodor, *Psychosemantics: The Prob-

lem of Meaning in the Philosophy of Mind (Cambridge: MIT Press, 1987), and *A Theory of Content and Other Essays* (Cambridge: MIT Press, 1990).

11. See Jaegwon Kim, "Concepts of Supervenience," *Philosophy and Phenomenological Research* 45 (1984), pp. 153–176.

12. The philosopher who made up this example is, of course, Hilary Putnam. See Putnam, "Meaning and Reference," and "The Meaning of 'Meaning'," in Putnam, *Mind, Language, and Reality.*

13. The author of this example is, of course, Tyler Burge. See Burge, "Individualism and the Mental," in P. French, T. Uehling, and H. Wettstein, eds., *Midwest Studies in Philosophy,* Vol. 5 (Minneapolis: University of Minnesota Press, 1979), pp. 73–122.

14. See John Searle, *Intentionality* (Cambridge: Cambridge University Press, 1983), and *The Rediscovery of the Mind* (Cambridge: MIT Press, 1992).

15. See Donald Davidson, "Knowing One's Own Mind," *Proceedings and Addresses of the American Philosophical Association* 60 (1986), pp. 441–458.

16. Davidson, "Knowing One's Own Mind," pp. 443–444.

17. See Hilary Putnam, *Reason, Truth, and History* (Cambridge: Cambridge University Press, 1981), p. 12.

Chapter 8

1. Rene Descartes, "The Passions of the Soul," in *The Philosophical Works of Descartes,* trans. by Elizabeth S. Haldane and G.R.T. Ross (Cambridge: Cambridge University Press, 1911), Articles 31 and 32. Reprinted in Brian Beakley and Peter Ludlow, eds., *The Philosophy of Mind: Classical Problems, Contemporary Issues* (Cambridge: MIT Press, 1992), pp. 111–112.

2. Descartes, "The Passions of the Soul," Articles 30 and 31.

3. Nicholas Malebranche, "The Union of Soul and Body," in *The Search After Truth,* trans. by Thomas Lennon and Paul Olscamp (Columbus: Ohio State University Press, 1980). Reprinted in Beakley and Ludlow, eds., *The Philosophy of Mind,* pp. 115–118.

4. See Gottfried Leibniz, "Monadology," in Steven M. Cahn, ed., *Classics of Western Philosophy,* 3d ed (Indianapolis: Hackett Publishing Co., 1977), pp. 604–613.

5. Leibniz, "Monadology," section 7.

6. Thomas Henry Huxley, "On the Hypothesis That Animals Are Automata," in Thomas Henry Huxley, *Collected Essays,* Vol. 1 (London, 1893). Reprinted in Beakley and Ludlow, eds., *The Philosophy of Mind,* pp. 133–136.

7. Jerry Fodor, "Making Mind Matter More," *Philosophical Topics* 17 (1989). Reprinted in Beakley and Ludlow, eds., *The Philosophy of Mind,* pp. 151–166, at p. 155.

8. The antecedent of a law is the part following the 'if' and preceding the 'then'. The consequent of a law is the part following the 'then'.

9. Jaegwon Kim, "The Non-Reductivist's Troubles with Mental Causation," in John Heil and Alfred Mele, eds., *Mental Causation* (Oxford: Clarendon Press, 1993), pp. 189–210, at p. 208.

10. Kim, "The Non-Reductivist's Troubles with Mental Causation," p. 202.

11. See Jaegwon Kim, "Multiple Realization and the Metaphysics of Reduction," *Philosophy and Phenomenological Research* 52, no. 1 (1992), pp. 1–26.

12. I am not so sure that moral properties really are a separate class; what we take to be moral properties supervening on states of affairs in the world may really be psychological properties supervening on *us*. But that is a topic for another book.

Chapter 9

1. From "Spirits in the Material World," by Sting. Used by permission of Criterion Music Corp.

2. Bertrand Russell, *The Problems of Philosophy* (New York: Oxford University Press, 1959), p. 161.

References

Baker, Lynne Rudder, *Saving Belief*. Princeton: Princeton University Press, 1987.

Beakley, Brian, and Ludlow, Peter, eds., *The Philosophy of Mind: Classical Problems, Contemporary Issues*. Cambridge: MIT Press, 1992.

Block, Ned, "The Computer Model of the Mind," in Osherson, D., and Smith, E. E., eds., *An Invitation to Cognitive Science*,Vol. 3, pp. 247–289. Cambridge: MIT Press, 1990.

———, "Troubles with Functionalism," in Beakley, Brian, and Ludlow, Peter, eds., *The Philosophy of Mind: Classical Problems, Contemporary Issues*, pp. 69–90. Cambridge: MIT Press, 1992.

Burge, Tyler, "Individualism and the Mental," in French, P., Uehling, T., and Wettstein, H., eds., *Midwest Studies in Philosophy*, Vol. 5, pp. 73–122. Minneapolis: University of Minnesota Press, 1979.

———, "Individualism and Psychology." *Philosophical Review* 95 (1986), pp. 3–46.

Cahn, Steven M., ed., *Classics of Western Philosophy*, 3d edition. Indianapolis: Hackett Publishing Co., 1977.

Churchland, Patricia, *Neurophilosophy: Toward a Unified Science of the Mind-Brain*. Cambridge: MIT Press, 1986.

———, "Reductionism and Antireductionism in Functionalist Theories of Mind," in Beakley, Brian, and Ludlow, Peter, eds., *The Philosophy of Mind: Classical Problems, Contemporary Issues,* pp. 59–67. Cambridge: MIT Press, 1992.

Churchland, Paul, "Eliminative Materialism and Propositional Attitudes." *Journal of Philosophy* 78 (1981), pp. 67–90.

———, *A Neurocomputational Perspective: The Nature of Mind and the Structure of Science*. Cambridge: MIT Press, 1989.

Cummins, Robert, "Functional Analysis." *Journal of Philosophy* 72 (1975), pp. 741–765.

Davidson, Donald, "Actions, Reasons, and Causes," in Davidson, Donald, *Essays on Actions and Events*, pp. 3–19. Oxford: Clarendon Press, 1980.

———, "Knowing One's Own Mind," *Proceedings and Addresses of the American Philosophical Association* 60 (1986), pp. 441–458.

———, "Mental Events," in Davidson, Donald, *Essays on Actions and Events*, pp. 207–227. Oxford: Clarendon Press, 1980.

———, "Reply to Essays X–XII," in Vermazen, Bruce, and Hintikka, Merrill, eds., *Essays on Davidson: Actions and Events*, pp. 242–252. Oxford: Oxford University Press, 1985.

Dennett, Daniel C., *The Intentional Stance*. Cambridge: MIT Press, 1987.

———, "Why the Law of Effect Will Not Go Away," *Journal of the Theory of Social Behavior* 5 (1974), pp. 169–187.

Descartes, Rene, *Meditations on First Philosophy*, trans. by Cress, Donald A. Indianapolis: Hackett Publishing Co., 1979.

———, "The Passions of the Soul," in *The Philosophical Works of Descartes*, trans. by Haldane and Ross. Cambridge: Cambridge University Press, 1911. Reprinted in Beakley, Brian, and Ludlow, Peter, eds., *The Philosophy of Mind: Classical Problems, Contemporary Issues*. Cambridge: MIT Press, 1992.

Devitt, Michael, and Sterelny, Kim, *Language and Reality: An Introduction to the Philosophy of Language*. Cambridge: MIT Press, 1987.

Dretske, Fred, *Explaining Behavior: Reasons in a World of Causes*. Cambridge: MIT Press, 1988.

———, *Knowledge and the Flow of Information*. Cambridge: MIT Press, 1981.

Evnine, Simon, *Donald Davidson*. Stanford: Stanford University Press, 1991.

Feigl, Herbert, "The 'Mental' and the 'Physical'," in *Minnesota Studies in the Philosophy of Science*, Vol. 2, pp. 474–485. Minneapolis: University of Minnesota Press, 1958.

Feinberg, Joel, "Action and Responsibility," in White, A., ed., *The Philosophy of Action*, pp. 95–119. Oxford: Oxford University Press, 1968.

Feyerabend, Paul, "Materialism and the Mind-Body Problem." *Review of Metaphysics* 17 (1963), pp. 49–66.

Fitzgerald, P. J., "Voluntary and Involuntary Acts," in White, A., ed., *The Philosophy of Action*. Oxford: Oxford University Press, 1968.

Fodor, Jerry, "The Appeal to Tacit Knowledge in Psychological Explanation." *Journal of Philosophy*, 65 (1968), pp. 627–640.

———, *The Language of Thought*. New York: Thomas Y. Crowell Co., reprinted by Harvard University Press, 1979.

———, "Making Mind Matter More," in Beakley, Brian, and Ludlow, Peter, eds., *The Philosophy of Mind: Classical Problems, Contemporary Issues*, pp. 151–166. Cambridge: MIT Press, 1992.

———, *Psychosemantics: The Problem of Meaning in the Philosophy of Mind*. Cambridge: MIT Press, 1987.

———, *A Theory of Content and Other Essays*. Cambridge: MIT Press, 1990.

Frege, Gottlob, "On Sense and Nominatum," in Martinich, A. P., ed., *The Philosophy of Language*, 2d edition, pp. 190–202. New York: Oxford University Press, 1990.

Hare, R. M., *The Language of Morals*. Oxford: Clarendon Press, 1952.

Heil, John, and Mele, Alfred, *Mental Causation*. Oxford: Clarendon Press, 1993.

Hempel, Carl G., *Aspects of Scientific Explanation*. New York: Free Press, 1965.

Hooker, C. A., "Towards a General Theory of Reduction," Parts 1, 2, and 3. *Dialogue* 20 (1981), pp. 38–59, 201–236, 496–529.

Horgan, Terence, and Woodward, James, "Folk Psychology Is Here to Stay." *Philosophical Review* 94 (1985), pp. 197–226.

Huxley, Thomas Henry, "On the Hypothesis That Animals Are Automata," in Huxley, Thomas Henry, *Collected Essays*, Vol. 1. London, 1893. Reprinted in Beakley, Brian, and Ludlow, Peter, eds., *The Philosophy of Mind: Classical Problems, Contemporary Issues*, pp. 133–136. Cambridge: MIT Press, 1992.

Jackson, Frank, and Pettit, Philip, "Some Content Is Narrow," in Heil, John, and Mele, Alfred, eds., *Mental Causation*, pp. 259–282. Oxford: Clarendon Press, 1993.

Kenny, Anthony, *The Metaphysics of Mind*. Oxford: Clarendon Press, 1989.

Kim, Jaegwon, "Concepts of Supervenience." *Philosophy and Phenomenological Research* 45 (1984), pp. 153–176.

———, "Multiple Realization and the Metaphysics of Reduction," *Philosophy and Phenomenological Research* 52, no. 1 (1992), pp. 1–26.

———, "The Non-Reductivist's Troubles with Mental Causation," in Heil, John, and Mele, Alfred, eds., *Mental Causation,* pp. 189–210. Oxford: Clarendon Press, 1993.

Kripke, Saul, "Identity and Necessity," in Beakley, Brian, and Ludlow, Peter, eds., *The Philosophy of Mind: Classical Problems, Contemporary Issues,* pp. 41–45. Cambridge: MIT Press, 1992.

———, *Naming and Necessity.* Cambridge: Cambridge University Press, 1972.

Leibniz, Gottfried, "Monadology," in Cahn, Steven M., ed., *Classics of Western Philosophy,* 3d edition, pp. 604–613. Indianapolis: Hackett Publishing Co., 1977.

Lewis, David, "How to Define Theoretical Terms," in Lewis, David, *Philosophical Papers,* Vol. 1, pp. 78–95. New York: Oxford University Press, 1983.

———, "Psychological and Theoretical Identification." *Australasian Journal of Philosophy,* 50 (1972), pp. 249–258.

Loar, Brian, "Subjective Intentionality." *Philosophical Topics* 15/1 (1987), pp. 89–124.

Lycan, William, *Consciousness.* Cambridge: MIT Press, 1987.

———, "Form, Function, and Feel." *Journal of Philosophy* 78 (1981), pp. 24–50.

———, "Towards a Homuncular Theory of Believing." *Cognition and Brain Theory* 4 (1981), pp. 139–159.

McCloskey, Michael, Caramazza, Alfonzo, and Green, Bert, "Curvilinear Motion in the Absence of External Forces: Naive Beliefs About the Motion of Objects." *Science* 210/4474 (1980), pp. 1139–1141.

———, "Intuitive Physics." *Scientific American* 248/4 (1983), pp. 122–130.

McGinn, Colin, Review of Patricia Churchland, *Neurophilosophy: Toward a Unified Science of the Mind-Brain* (Cambridge: MIT Press, 1987). *Times Literary Supplement,* Feb. 6, 1987.

Malebranche, Nicholas, "The Union of Soul and Body," in *The Search After Truth,* trans. by Lennon, Thomas, and Olscamp, Paul. Columbus: Ohio State University Press, 1980. Reprinted in Beakley, Brian, and Ludlow, Peter, eds., *The Philosophy of Mind: Classical Problems, Contemporary Issues,* pp. 115–118. Cambridge: MIT Press, 1992.

Martinich, A. P., ed., *The Philosophy of Language,* 1st edition. New York: Oxford University Press, 1985.

———, ed., *The Philosophy of Language,* 2d edition. New York: Oxford University Press, 1990.

Melden, A. I., *Free Action.* London: Routledge and Kegan Paul, 1961.

Millikan, Ruth, *Language, Thought, and Other Biological Categories.* Cambridge: MIT Press, 1984.

Moore, G. E., "The Conception of Intrinsic Value," in Moore, G. E., *Philosophical Studies.* Paterson, N. J.: Littlefield, Adams, and Co., 1959.

Nagel, Ernest, *The Structure of Science.* New York: Harcourt, Brace, and World, 1961.

Nisbett, Richard E., and Wilson, Timothy D., "Telling More Than We Can Know: Verbal Reports on Mental Processes." *Psychological Review* 84 (1977), pp. 231–259.

Place, U. T., "Is Consciousness a Brain Process?" *British Journal of Psychology* 47 (1956), pp. 44–50.

Plato, *Meno*, trans. by Grube, G.M.A., in Cahn, Stephen M., ed., *Classics of Western Philosophy*, 3d edition, pp. 4–27. Indianapolis: Hackett Publishing Co., 1977.

Putnam, Hilary, "Brains in a Vat," in Putnam, Hilary, *Reason, Truth, and History*, pp. 1–21. Cambridge: Cambridge University Press, 1981.

———, "Meaning and Reference." *Journal of Philosophy* 70 (1973), pp. 699–711.

———, "The Meaning of 'Meaning'," in Putnam, Hilary, *Mind, Language, and Reality: Philosophical Papers*, Vol. 2, pp. 215–271. New York: Cambridge University Press, 1975.

———, "The Nature of Mental States," in Beakley, Brian, and Ludlow, Peter, eds., *The Philosophy of Mind: Classical Problems, Contemporary Issues*, pp. 51–58. Cambridge: MIT Press, 1992.

———, "Philosophy and Our Mental Life," in Beakley, Brian, and Ludlow, Peter, eds., *The Philosophy of Mind: Classical Problems, Contemporary Issues*, pp. 91–99. Cambridge: MIT Press, 1992.

———, *Reason, Truth, and History.* Cambridge: Cambridge University Press, 1981.

———, *Representation and Reality.* Cambridge: MIT Press, 1988.

Pylyshyn, Zenon, *Computation and Cognition.* Cambridge: MIT Press, 1984.

Quine, W.V.O., *Word and Object.* Cambridge: MIT Press, 1960.

Rescher, Nicholas, *Scientific Explanation.* New York: Free Press, 1970.

Rorty, Richard, "In Defense of Eliminative Materialism." *Review of Metaphysics* 24 (1970), pp. 112–121.

Russell, Bertrand, "Descriptions," in Martinich, A. P., ed., *The Philosophy of Language*, 1st edition. New York: Oxford University Press, 1985.

———, *The Problems of Philosophy.* New York: Oxford University Press, 1959.

Ryle, Gilbert, *The Concept of Mind.* New York: Barnes and Noble, 1949.

Schiffer, Stephen, "Physicalism." *Philosophical Perspectives* 4 (1990), pp. 153–185.

———, *Remnants of Meaning.* Cambridge: MIT Press, 1987.

Searle, John, "Indeterminacy, Empiricism, and the First Person." *Journal of Philosophy* 84/3 (1987), pp. 123–146.

———, *Intentionality.* Cambridge: Cambridge University Press, 1983.

———, "Minds, Brains, and Programs." *Behavioral and Brain Sciences* 3 (1980), pp. 417–458.

———, *The Rediscovery of the Mind.* Cambridge: MIT Press, 1992.

Smart, J.J.C, "Sensations and Brain Processes." *Philosophical Review* 68 (1959), pp. 141–156.

Sterelny, Kim, *The Representational Theory of Mind: An Introduction.* Cambridge: Basil Blackwell, 1991.

Stich, Stephen, *From Folk Psychology to Cognitive Science: The Case Against Belief.* Cambridge: MIT Press, 1983.

Turing, Alan, "Computing Machinery and Intelligence." *Mind* 59 (1950), pp. 433–460.

Vermazen, Bruce, and Hintikka, Merrill, eds., *Essays on Davidson: Actions and Events*. Oxford: Oxford University Press, 1985.
Watson, Gary, *Free Will*. Oxford: Oxford University Press, 1982.
Weizenbaum, J., *Computer Power and Human Reason*. San Francisco: W. H. Freeman, 1976.
White, Alan R., *The Philosophy of Action*. Oxford: Oxford University Press, 1968.

About the Book and Author

CONTEMPORARY PHILOSOPHY has seen a proliferation of complex theories and intricate arguments brought to bear on the mind-body problem, perhaps the most intractable of perennial philosophical problems. In this concise and accessible text, Barbara Hannan provides an elegant introduction to this contemporary debate.

Her emphasis is upon the clear and even-handed presentation and evaluation of the major theories of the mind, but she does not shrink from contributing to the advancement of the argument, including the presentation of an original account, the theory of "content internalism." Along the way to the formulation of this account, Hannan puts into context and discusses the views of all the major contemporary philosophers writing on the mind, including Lewis, Putnam, Searle, Davidson, Dennett, and Fodor.

Combining a deep respect for the depth of the issues with clarity of thought and lucidity of expression, *Subjectivity and Reduction* is the ideal introduction to the central problem of today's philosophy of mind.

BARBARA HANNAN is assistant professor of philosophy at the University of New Mexico. She has taught previously at the University of Arkansas and the University of Idaho.

Index